We Rode the Orphan Trains

We Rode the Orphan Trains

Andrea Warren

CLARION BOOKS
AN IMPRINT OF HARPERCOLLINS*PUBLISHERS*
BOSTON NEW YORK

For information, address HarperCollins Publishers, 195 Broadway, New York, NY 10007.

www.harpercollinschildrens.com

Book design by Lisa Diercks
The text of this book is set in Clifford Eighteen.

Library of Congress Cataloging-in-Publication Data

Warren, Andrea.
We rode the orphan trains / Andrea Warren.
p. cm.
Includes bibliographical references.
RNF ISBN 0-618-11712-1 PAP ISBN 0-618-43235-3
1. Orphan trains—Juvenile literature. 2. Orphans—United States—Biography—Juvenile literature.
[1. Orphan trains. 2. Orphans.] I. Title.
HV985.W39 2001
362.73'4'0973—dc21

Manufactured in Vietnam

23 RRDA 20 19 18 17 16 15 14

For Lee Nailling, 1917–2001,

who rode an orphan train to Texas in 1926,

for Alice Bullis Ayler,

an orphan train rider who met every obstacle

with grit and grace,

for my adopted daughter, Alison Doerr,

whose "orphan train" was an airplane from South Vietnam

to the United States of America in April 1975,

and for children of all ages who know

that real *family does not have to be biological*

Acknowledgments

I AM GRATEFUL TO my agent, Regina Ryan; my editor, Kim Keller, at Houghton Mifflin; Mary Ellen Johnson and the Orphan Train Heritage Society of America; Phil Coltoff and Vic Remer at the Children's Aid Society; my writing buddies, Barbara Bartocci and Deborah Shouse; my husband, Jay Wiedenkeller, who is always patient, always interested; and to all the orphan train riders who generously contributed their memories to this book.

Contents

We Rode the Orphan Trains

Orphan trains followed the ever-expanding railroad tracks. This train carried its special cargo of orphan train riders around the year 1900. KANSAS STATE HISTORICAL SOCIETY

Introduction

WHEN MY FIRST BOOK about the orphan trains, *Orphan Train Rider: One Boy's True Story,* was published, readers told me that they were hungry for more stories about real-life riders. I heard this so often, I decided to write a second book. I made the decision to tell the stories of riders still living so that I could capture the immediacy of their experiences, just as I did in *Orphan Train Rider,* which chronicles the journey of nine-year-old Lee Nailling.

Several hundred riders are still alive, and the hardest thing I had to do was decide whom to interview for this book. Many have incredible stories. Like all of the riders, those whose stories you are about to read are remarkable people. Each is unique, yet all share much in common beyond the fact of having ridden an orphan train. Each rider has struggled with feelings of abandonment and inferiority. All eight have devoted their later years to speaking to schoolchildren and community groups about their experiences, and they know that hearing this history from someone who lived it has tremendous impact on listeners.

I hope you will enjoy their stories.

CHAPTER 1

Homes for Homeless Children

SHORTLY AFTER HER BIRTH in 1922, Lorraine Williams was put in a New York City orphanage; she was there until she was four. Lorraine still has vivid memories of being hungry. "Each child was given a shallow tin pie pan to eat from. Dinner was a bowl of thin soup with vegetables in it, and we got one ladle each. I was always hungry," she recalls.

"I was very small for my age, and I was quiet. Mostly I looked and listened, but I knew how to watch out for myself. One day I got brave enough to ask, 'Please, may I have more?' I can still see the angry look on the matron's face as she hit my arm, telling me I could have no more. I did not cry. Orphans learn not to cry."

In 1926 Lorraine and thirteen other orphans were placed in the custody of an organization called the Children's Aid Society. They were scrubbed clean, dressed in new clothes, and put aboard a passenger train at Grand Central Station. The agents traveling with the children did not want to upset them and thought it was best not to tell them where they were going or why.

The kids did not know that they were on an "orphan train" and were participating in the largest children's migration in history.

Between 1854 and 1929 an estimated two hundred thousand American children, some orphaned or half-orphaned, others abandoned—but all in need of families—traveled west by rail as part of a "placing out" program started by the Children's Aid Society of New York City. Eventually other organizations got involved as well. These charitable groups removed children from unsatisfactory circumstances, such as the slums of New York City, and took them to rural areas to try to find them new homes and families.

When Lorraine's train reached Kirksville, Missouri, the children were taken to a local church crowded with people. The children were told to sit in chairs on the stage. An old man with a white beard approached Lorraine, who was a small, fair-haired child, and pointed a bony finger at her. "I'll take that one!" he boomed. "My wife is sick and I need someone to wash the dishes."

"I whimpered and pulled back," Lorraine remembers. "My instincts told me not to go with him. J. W. Swan, the agent who had traveled with us, told me I did not have to."

"But she's the one I want!" the old man insisted, looming over her.

When a couple standing nearby saw what was happening, the husband dashed to an ice-cream shop and returned with a strawberry cone.

> He knelt in front of me and asked, "Would you like to have this?" His voice was very gentle. "You can have one every day," he told me. An orphan never turns down food and I took the cone. I can still remember how good it tasted. I put my hand in his hand. He turned to his wife and said, "Minnie, let's take this little girl home."

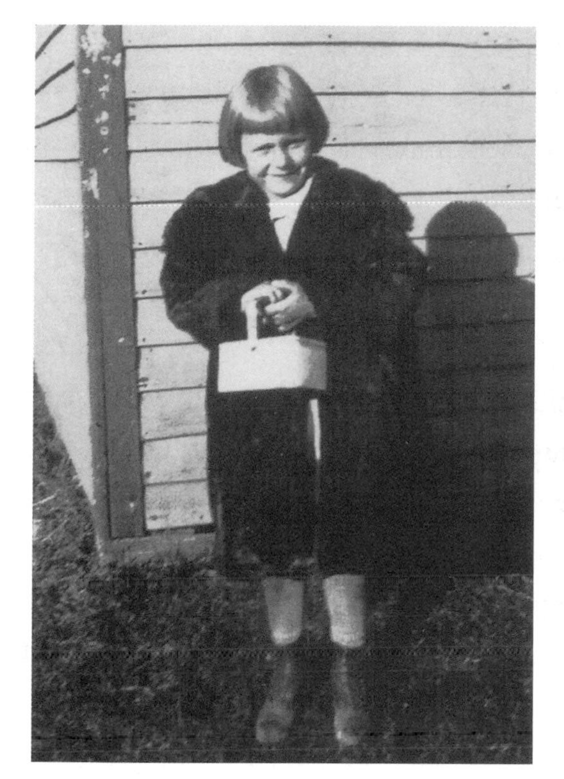

Left: Lorraine Williams was six years old and happily settled in her new home when this photo was taken. LORRAINE WILLIAMS *Right:* Lorraine Williams has been an active volunteer for many causes that benefit children. She was even honored at the White House by First Lady Barbara Bush for her work promoting literacy. LORRAINE WILLIAMS

I could not have had more loving parents. I had no desire to ever meet my birth mother. I learned some years ago that she put me in the orphanage because her fiancé had died and she feared the wrath of her prominent family if they found out she had a baby. My adoptive parents are the ones who wanted and loved me. If I go to heaven, my eyes will search only for them. They gave me life.

Not all of the children who rode orphan trains found so happy a home at the end of their journey. Some suffered abuse, were treated like hired help, or were never fully accepted by their new families. Officials knew that the placing out program was imperfect and did what they could to screen out inappropriate families. But in spite of problems, placing out provided the best chance many of the children had of finding a home.

EARLY IN AMERICA'S HISTORY, children who lost their parents were usually raised by relatives or neighbors. But beginning in about 1830, this practice no longer worked. The problem of homeless children mushroomed in large cities in the East, particularly in New York City.

In 1850, when New York City's population was 500,000, an estimated 10,000 to 30,000 homeless children lived on the streets or were warehoused in orphanages. Some children were orphaned when their parents died in epidemics of typhoid, yellow fever, or the flu. Many were the sons and daughters of down-on-their-luck immigrants flooding into the city from Europe. Every day, children were abandoned or orphaned by parents who fell victim to the grinding poverty of the slums and high rates of drug and alcohol addiction. The Civil War also left countless children without fathers. If they subsequently lost their mothers, they had to rely on relatives for help or ended up fending for themselves.

Few social services existed to help struggling families or to rescue suffering children. Orphanages were too few in number and often grossly overcrowded. Children in orphanages typically received minimal food, education, and attention. By age fourteen they were expected to leave and to make their own way in life.

As a young man, Charles Loring Brace started the Children's Aid Society to help New York City's destitute children. He was twenty-nine years old when this photo was taken.
ORPHAN TRAIN HERITAGE SOCIETY OF AMERICA

A minister and reformer named Charles Loring Brace founded the Children's Aid Society in 1853 to help destitute children in New York City. Brace was just twenty-two when he started working in a mission house in the worst slum in the city. He saw the thousands of children who had no adults to care for them, no families to love them. Some children sold rags or matches, trying to earn a few pennies to buy bread. Others became thieves and pickpockets. They slept wherever they could, on sidewalk steam grates,

In 1890, this group of Children's Aid Society boys paused for a photo before leaving for the station to catch their train west to new homes. They were sponsored by a wealthy patron, Mrs. John Jacob Astor. JACOB A. RIIS COLLECTION, MUSEUM OF THE CITY OF NEW YORK

in makeshift shacks, or under bridges. Brace's heart went out to these waifs. Through his society, he established services to help them. He opened lodging houses for newsboys and set up schools to teach children trades or occupations to support themselves. He sent physicians and nurses into the slums to offer medical care, started a daycare center for the children of mothers who had to work, and made it possible for poor children to receive free school lunches. Some of his programs are still in existence today.

Brace was especially interested in trying to find homes for the crush of homeless children living on the streets. He felt that any child was better off with a family than in an institution. He had traveled in Europe, where he had learned about small groups of orphans taken by charitable organizations to areas where they stood the best chance of finding families who would raise them as their own. He also knew of various experimental programs both in the United States and abroad to secure placements for children.

He decided to try the concept of placing out as a way to find homes for some of the homeless children in New York City. In the beginning he settled children with families in upstate New York, but the need for families was so great that he looked toward the West. He felt that goodhearted families in small towns and on farms would take the children, educate them, and see that they had a religious upbringing. In return, it was understood that the children would contribute their labor to the family. This was expected of any child at that time, when all but the most privileged youngsters helped with daily chores.

In 1854 Brace sent the first group—forty-six children in all—to Michigan. Within a week of arrival, they all had homes. Soon thousands of children were being placed out. They came from the streets, and even from jail.

They came out of orphanages with names like the Howard Mission and Home for Little Wanderers, the New York Home for Friendless Boys, and Mother Theodore's Memorial Girls' Home. Sometimes parents brought their children to Brace, hoping that they would have more opportunity out West. Some children found Brace on their own. All had to be signed into the custody of the society before they could make the journey. Then they were dressed in new clothing, given a Bible, and placed in the care of society agents who accompanied them on the trip.

Trains became the primary means of transportation, with trips usually lasting a few days to a week or more. Most children thought the train ride was an adventure, but few understood what was happening to them. Once they did, their reactions ranged from excitement at finding a new family to concern that they were being placed with families when they knew that they had relatives "back home."

Because the majority of placements worked out well, the numbers of children riding the trains continued to grow. Brace raised money to support the program through his writings and speeches. Wealthy people occasionally stepped forward to sponsor whole trainloads of children (causing critics of the program to charge that their real goal was to get the "riffraff" off the streets). Railroads helped out by offering discount fares. Posters were put up in towns along the way to announce when a train was coming. Local committees were formed to approve applications of families wanting a child.

ORPHAN TRAIN RIDERS WENT to every state in the Union, but most went to the Midwest. Since this area was settled primarily by immigrants from western Europe, most of the children who rode the trains were white. Society

Homes Wanted

FOR CHILDREN.

A Company of Orphan Children of different ages will arrive at

Oakland, Iowa,
Friday, Dec. 9, '04.

The Distribution will take place at the Opera House at 10:30 a.m. and 1:30 p.m.

The object of the coming of these children is to find homes in your midst, especially among farmers, where they may enjoy a happy and wholesome family life, where kind care, good example and moral training will fit them for a life of self-support and usefulness. They come under the auspices of the New York Children's Aid Society, by whom they have been tested and found to be well-meaning and willing boys and girls.

The conditions are that these children shall be properly clothed, treated as members of the family, given proper school advantages and remain in the family until they are eighteen years of age. At the expiration of the time specified it is hoped that arrangements can be made whereby they may be able to remain in the family indefinitely. The Society retains the right to remove a child at any time for just cause and agrees to remove any found unsatisfactory after being notified.

Applications may be made to any one of the following well known citizens, who have agreed to act as local committee to aid the agent in securing homes.

Committee: S. S. Rust, E. M. Smart, A. C. Vieth, E. C. Read, W. B. Batler, Dr. R. G. Smith, N. W. Wentz.

Remember the time and place. All are invited. Come out and hear the address.

Office: 105 East 22d St., New York City.

H. D. CLARK, Iowa Agent,
Dodge Center, Minn.

Posters put up in towns to advertise the coming of an orphan train included as much information as possible about terms and conditions for taking the children. CHILDREN'S AID SOCIETY

These neatly groomed orphan train riders were headed for Sweet Springs, Missouri, in 1909. CHILDREN'S AID SOCIETY

officials believed that children with ethnic and religious backgrounds similar to the families who would be considering them had the best chance of finding homes.

Placing children older than fourteen was always difficult because people feared that such youngsters were too set in their ways or might have bad habits, like smoking or stealing. It was easiest to find homes for babies, and hardest to find homes for children who were sickly, or physically or mentally handicapped.

Usually a group of thirty to forty children traveled together, though their numbers could be as small as three and on a few occasions exceeded a hundred. When an orphan train arrived in a town, everyone turned out for the "viewing." Many riders recalled with horror how prospective parents examined and questioned them.

As Hazelle Latimer, now deceased, who rode an orphan train to Texas in 1918, remembered, "We were lined up on the stage and all I could see was wall-to-wall people. They surrounded us, made us turn around, lift our skirts to see if our legs were straight, and open our mouths to show our teeth. A very humiliating day."

Adoption was not a common practice in the United States until after 1900, when it became necessary for legal reasons that included the inheritance of property. Children taken before that time usually remained foster children, though they would normally take their new family's last name and were considered part of the family. Many of the children felt the stigma of being an orphan their entire lives. Some felt unwanted by their birth parents and not fully accepted by their new parents. Some were the targets of teasing, name-calling, and ridicule from schoolmates and townspeople. For these reasons, some riders never told their own children about their pasts, ashamed that they had been "train riders."

Some matches between the riders and their new families did not work well. Agents who worked for the society tried to follow up with yearly visits to check on the children and to remove those who were in unfit homes, and some were moved several times before they found good homes. Claretta Miller, now deceased, was one of these children. She had no good memories of life with her birth mother. She and her two sisters were sickly, undernourished, and covered with lice, and they slept on dirty mattresses on the floor. At night rats ran over their beds. Claretta never forgot the times she would awaken, screaming, when a rat got entangled in her hair. When the girls were taken from their alcoholic mother by New York state authorities, Claretta was placed first in foster care, then in an orphanage.

She was sent west in 1918 with two hundred other children on an orphan train, and in Omaha she was taken by a German family who already had nine children and were looking for a servant. When she was removed from that home, she went to another foster home, and then to another, where she became ill with the flu. It took her months to fully recover. In writing about her life, she described herself at eight years old as a "lost and lonely little girl."

Then a Nebraska farmer and his wife agreed to take her. "I arrived by horse and buggy at the Carman farm after dark on a rainy night," she recalled. "When I was put to bed that night, the floodgates opened wide and I cried my heart out. Mrs. Carman had never had any children of her own. She had a heart as big as all outdoors. She stayed with me until the tears were over and I at last fell fast asleep."

Claretta found a happy home with the Carmans and grew to adulthood with them. Like most orphan train riders, she looked back on her trip west as a blessing.

Not all children were taken by families. When a group of Catholic nuns, the Sisters of Saint Francis, in Oldenburg, Indiana, heard in 1898 of the need for homes for children, they took three small girls and reared them at their convent, sewing all their clothes and educating them at the convent school.

Some children were taken only for their labor. In 1888 thirty boys between the ages of ten and fifteen who resided in a Brooklyn orphanage were sent to a glassworks factory in Ohio in need of cheap laborers. Other children were taken as farm hands or kitchen drudges. Many were expected to live in attics or barns, and were not allowed to go to school. Some of the children were physically, emotionally, and sexually abused.

But mostly placing out worked well. Orphanages in various states sponsored orphan trains, sending children anywhere from a few miles to a few states away in search of homes.

The New York Foundling Hospital was second to the Children's Aid Society in placing children. In 1869 the Sisters of Charity, headed by Sister Irene, began caring for abandoned infants and toddlers at the newly created Foundling Hospital in New York City. In those days a "hospital" could mean a place where people received care other than medical. The sisters put a cradle in a protected area near the front door where infants could be left. Some people offered no information about the child. Others wrote out the child's name and birth date. And some left notes for the sisters. One read, "It is a heartbroken mother who is compelled to surrender her child through misfortune." Another said, "Augustus, born October 16, 1879. Take good care of my darling." Yet another implored, "My wife, its mother, is dead. Do the very best you can do for my little one."

Soon the sisters were overwhelmed with children. Believing, like Brace, that the best situation for a child was a home, they sent many of their small charges west to preassigned Catholic homes. Even though all the children

A rare photo taken around 1890 shows Sister Irene with children who lived at her New York Foundling Hospital. JACOB A. RIIS COLLECTION, MUSEUM OF THE CITY OF NEW YORK

The old Foundling Hospital, since replaced, where mothers could leave their children when they could not care for them, was a massive Victorian building in New York City.

ORPHAN TRAIN HERITAGE SOCIETY OF AMERICA

were spoken for, the arrival in town of a "baby train" was always of great interest, drawing huge crowds who came to watch the children united with their new parents.

Peg Kildare, now deceased, whose birth mother turned her over to the Foundling Hospital when she was three weeks old and never made further inquiry of her, rode a baby train in 1921 to Norfolk, Nebraska, when she was twenty-two months old. Her new parents had one son, who was nineteen; they had lost six other children.

Everett Jansen Wendell, a wealthy trustee of the Children's Aid Society, sometimes accompanied small groups of orphan train riders looking for new homes. He was beloved by the children, who called him "Pops." In 1910, this little company was leaving New York City by boat for Delaware and Maryland. CHILDREN'S AID SOCIETY

In recalling her history, Peg wrote of her arrival, "Mother said that people came from all around the surrounding towns. Many just to see what sort of a thing was going on. Mother said many folks who were to get a child brought their friends as well as their families. . . . The nun placed me in Mother's arms and said, 'Here's your little girl, be good to her.' She needn't have concerned herself, for they certainly were good to me and gave me much love and affection, just as if I had been born to them."

Though both the Foundling Hospital and the Children's Aid Society tried very hard to place brothers and sisters in the same home or at least in the same area—and there are stories of as many as seven siblings being kept together—sometimes this was not possible. The separation of brothers and sisters was always wrenching.

Orphan train rider Robert Baker, who is deceased, recalled that when the group of children he was with was put on a stage in Palmyra, Missouri, in 1927, "We felt like a bunch of cattle, as we heard voices saying, 'I'll take that one' or 'I'll take this one.' Can you imagine what we were going through?... For the first time, my brother Dick and I were separated. What a cruel world!"

Jack Voigt felt the same way. He and his two sisters rode an orphan train to Kansas in 1920. When the children were lined up, Voigt wrote in his memoir, "It was like picking out puppies." His older sister found a good home with a family in another part of the state. His younger sister was taken by a family and never heard from again. Voigt went home with a family who decided a year later not to keep him. He was then placed in a second home, where he was worked hard and beaten regularly. He ran away at age twelve and went to live with his older sister and her new family.

Emily Lung's big brother Henry was all she had in the world. She held on tight to him while two families fought over them in Warrensburg, Missouri, in 1913. One family wanted only her. The other family, the O'Briens, wanted both children, and they eventually won. Emily's name was changed to Millie and she and her brother received a good home and both were legally adopted.

In 1904, a group of older boys paused for a photo once they were on board their train and ready to leave to find new homes in Texas. CHILDREN'S AID SOCIETY

Often siblings were separated before the journey, when at least one was left behind. Sylvia Wemhoff of Humphrey, Nebraska, was put aboard an orphan train in New York City in 1918 when she was an infant. She was a grandmother before she was able to obtain a copy of her birth certificate, and from it she learned that she had a sibling. Her story appeared on the television show *Unsolved Mysteries* in 1989, and as a result, she was reunited with her older brother, Joseph Volk.

The orphan trains stopped running in 1930 for several reasons, including a decreased need for farm labor in the Midwest and the onset of the Great

These young children about to leave from the Foundling Hospital on baby trains could not have known what was ahead of them. CORBIS IMAGES

Depression. Many states were questioning the propriety of accepting children from other states. Also, social service agencies had begun temporarily placing children from troubled families in foster homes, with the goal of restoring them to their families as soon as possible. For immigrants, the transition to life in America became a little easier. New programs helped them get jobs and housing when they first arrived. Thus fewer children from these families were given up by their parents.

Today the Orphan Train Heritage Society of America (OTHSA), headquartered in Springdale, Arkansas, helps spread the word about the orphan trains, a relatively unknown topic in American history. The society sponsors an annual reunion for riders, as do some states, and these events draw riders, their families, and people interested in the orphan trains. The riders still alive are elderly, and the society is striving to find them and to record their stories.

According to Mary Ellen Johnson, executive director of OTHSA, which she founded in 1987, "Most riders knew little or nothing of their pasts either because of lack of information or because their adoption records were sealed. Some found good homes and some did not.

"Having ridden an orphan train sets them apart in a way the rest of us can never understand. They are like family to each other."

The recollections of Hazelle Latimer, Claretta Miller, Peg Kildare, Robert Baker, Jack Voigt, and Emily Lung, all deceased, appear in materials published by OTHSA. Lorraine Williams was interviewed from her home in Temple Hills, Maryland, and Sylvia Wemhoff from her home in Humphrey, Nebraska.

CHAPTER 2

Agent Clara Comstock's Mission

EVEN IN THE DARK OF night, Clara Comstock slept very little when she rode one of the orphan trains. As the agent in charge, she remained alert to any unusual sounds from the children sleeping curled up on the seats around her: a child having a nightmare, or one who was cold and needed another blanket. A cough that could be soothed with medicine, or an older boy or girl lying wide awake who wanted to talk.

Art Smith rode an orphan train to Iowa in 1922 with Miss Comstock. He felt protected in her care. "She was a very loving person," he recalls, "very sweet and motherly. She took a personal interest in each child she took west, and even though I was only four years old at the time, I knew she would look after me. She was quick to wipe away tears, and quick with comfort and reassurance. I knew right away she was a very special lady."

Miss Comstock was one of many agents who worked for the Children's Aid Society through the years, helping to place the children with good families. In a presentation to the Society staff in 1931, she explained the respon-

Clara Comstock was so highly regarded by the Children's Aid Society that in 1957 they honored her at a special retirement luncheon, the event where this photo was taken. She died in 1963. CHILDREN'S AID SOCIETY

sibilities handled by the agents. When she was ready to take a group of children west, she visited orphanages and charitable agencies in the New York City area, selecting children she felt certain she could find homes for. This could be a heartbreaking task when a child who seemed unsuitable begged to be taken along.

Once children were selected to go on an orphan train, they were cleaned up and outfitted in new clothing. PRIVATE COLLECTION OF ANNA LAURA HILL, COURTESY OF THE ORPHAN TRAIN HERITAGE SOCIETY OF AMERICA

Once the children were selected, she brought them to the Children's Aid Society in New York City, where they were scrubbed clean, given haircuts, and outfitted with two sets of new clothes: one to wear on the train, the other to put on when they met prospective parents. As Miss Comstock reported, "The children were very happy about their clothing and admired themselves all the way west, and often insisted on wearing their gloves the entire distance."

In addition to selecting and readying the children, the agents filled a trunk with extra clothing for the children. They packed up food in large boxes, bringing such things as bread, peanut butter, jelly, ham, cheese, celery, and cookies, and condensed milk for the very young children. Fresh fruit and milk were purchased along the way. They also brought such items as toothpaste, soap, washcloths and towels, silverware, bibs for the babies, medicine, and sewing supplies. Agents packed personal bags for themselves, since they might be gone for as long as six weeks.

The day of the journey, the children were taken to the train station by streetcar, with older children helping to look after the younger ones. Agents carried the babies. At the train station, the children were loaded before the other passengers boarded, filling the back part of a car or even a whole car. Sometimes children were malnourished and needed extra attention. Agents did their best to assure that the children were healthy when they arrived. When time permitted, they worked with children on their manners and other ways to make good impressions. Sometimes they read stories or sang to them.

The nuns, nurses, and agents who accompanied very young children on the baby trains sponsored by the Foundling Hospital, and the caretakers who traveled with children from other sponsoring agencies, were usually among several adults aboard who were responsible for the children. Some agents made the journey alone. W. C. Van Meter, who was an agent with the Children's Aid Society (and was arrested in Illinois in 1857 on charges of bringing "paupers" into the state), recalled a seven-day journey he made by himself with twenty-seven children, traveling from New York to Illinois. But usually two agents assumed the responsibility for a group that large. Sometimes Miss Comstock traveled with Anna Laura Hill, an agent who became her good friend.

For agents traveling alone, changing trains in Chicago or St. Louis was difficult. According to Miss Comstock, "If two agents were along, this was not hard, for one would go ahead and the other follow with the children between.

Four-year-old Ruth Thomas and her seven-year-old sister, Blanche, traveled on an orphan train from an orphanage in upstate New York to Sulphur Springs, Texas, in 1918. Blanche lived in several homes and another orphanage before she found a family. Ruth took another train to the small Texas town of Weatherford, where she found a home. In the photo with her on the day she was taken from the train in Weatherford is her new mother, Mrs. Abbey Raper, agent Emil Recke, who cared for her on the trip, and an unidentified man.

BETTY GLIDEWELL, DAUGHTER OF BLANCHE THOMAS BRAXTON, NIECE OF RUTH THOMAS RAPER

These children, newly arrived in Lebanon, Missouri, in December 1909 and not yet selected by families, were accompanied on their journey by agents B. W. Tice and Anna Laura Hill, who was Clara Comstock's close friend. CHILDREN'S AID SOCIETY

Each agent had a baby in her arms usually, and the baggage was distributed among the older children if no porters were available. The older children were always helpful on the train."

Train personnel and passengers frequently volunteered their help. Many were interested in what was happening to the children and often bought treats for them.

Some groups made stops along the way, staying only long enough for townspeople to look over the children and perhaps take one home. If possible, when they reached their destination, the group went to a hotel to rest and clean up before the viewing. After the children were placed in homes, agents stayed on a few days to make sure that everything was satisfactory, and to visit children previously placed in the area. Some children lived in isolated settings, and agents found themselves using any possible means of transportation to make their yearly visits, including horse and buggy, boats, and even sleighs.

Miss Comstock said about those early days before automobiles:

> We sat up in the wind and storm under a top buggy, the thermometer ranging from 36 degrees below zero to 113 degrees above. . . . There were few bridges, and if floods came, we forded the streams or stayed where we were. The hotels were very poor, the food inedible. Women were received with suspicion if they traveled alone at night and some hotels refused them admission. . . . In the wild hay country of northern Nebraska, there were no roads, you angled across the prairie. Once, I got lost on the prairie on a cold November night. . . . The driver was a one-eyed man and could not see the trail, and I was too much of a tenderfoot to know it.

Miss Comstock reported that she sometimes stayed in one place for two weeks. She also recalled once spending three weeks quarantined in a "dreary hotel room" caring for a five-year-old ill with diphtheria.

The children remembered the agents with both fear and fondness. One rider likened the agent on his train to a witch. Another compared his to an angel. Some of the children and agents stayed in touch for decades. Most agents had backgrounds as teachers, social workers, or ministers and were committed to the children and their welfare, and physically strong enough to withstand the grueling travel involved in placing and visiting the children.

"Miss Comstock made friends with people in the towns she visited," Art Smith says, "but she would be firm with them when necessary. If she thought a child was being mistreated, she would remove the child from that home in an instant."

Clara Comstock had started her career in 1903 as a teacher at the Brace Farm School before she became interested in becoming an agent—a position she held between 1911 and 1928. After that, she continued to work for the Children's Aid Society for nearly two more decades. In all, she made seventy-four trips on the orphan trains.

She was highly regarded by everyone at the Children's Aid Society, according to Victor Remer, CAS's archivist. "I recall a letter she wrote to a colleague telling how she had used part of her vacation entertaining 'her kids,'" Remer said. "Clara wrote, 'It was a pleasure to have them.' I was deeply moved by this. It was typical of her, for she was a real mother surrogate to all of her children."

Miss Comstock acknowledged that she grew attached to the children in her care. "To be an agent, she gave up the possibility of marriage and a family of her own," says Art Smith. "I think we children were her extended family. Long after she retired, she stayed in touch with many riders."

She summed up her responsibilities as an agent when she wrote, "The work was a great adventure in Faith; we were always helped and grew to expect kindness, deep interest, and assistance everywhere. We were constantly attempting the impossible. . . . I thought it was the most incredible thing imaginable to expect people to take children they had never seen and to give them a home, but we placed them and never failed to accomplish it."

Information from Clara Comstock's presentation to the Children's Aid Society staff in 1931 is used by permission of the CAS. Interview information for Art Smith can be found on page 79.

CHAPTER 3

Twins Who Just Wanted to Be Loved

Nettie and Nellie Crook, Riders to Kansas, 1911

NETTIE ENNS AND HER identical twin, Nellie, were born Nettie and Nellie Crook in 1905. Their birthdays were actually a day apart: Nellie was born before midnight on January 23 and Nettie in the wee hours of January 24. They had an older brother, Leon, and soon a younger sister. From the earliest Nettie can remember, her mother was always leaving. Mrs. Crook, their mother, who had married and started her family when she was sixteen, may have felt overwhelmed. Or maybe there was another reason she frequently left her husband and children in upstate New York to visit her family back in Vermont. Nettie does not know. She remembers that her father, too, was often away from home for work. For a while he was a dredger on the Erie Canal.

The family moved often. One apartment Nettie can recall had an outside staircase. Her father and his friends used to sit around the kitchen table drinking beer and having a good time. She also remembers when her little sister died of an illness—an awful time for everyone. "She was lying so still in her coffin and candles were burning at either end," Nettie remembers. "We were all very sad. I have always felt terrible about it."

Perhaps it was this event that triggered her mother's depression, leading her to abuse and neglect the twins and Leon. Nettie isn't sure, and neither Leon nor Nellie would talk about it when they were alive.

The authorities became involved in the family's situation, and in 1910, when the twins were five and Leon was nine, the local justice of the peace came to the door with official papers and informed Nettie's mother that the children were to go with him. He had a horse-drawn wagon outside and told the children to get in. Their father was not home, and Nettie does not remember her mother trying to stop the man.

She never saw her mother again. In slightly over a year's time, she and Nellie and Leon had lost their little sister and then their mother and father.

THE THREE CHILDREN WERE taken to an orphanage in Kingston, New York. There, they were told to not look back. "We knew to mind adults, so we did not ask questions," Nettie says. "Their goal was to give us a new life. They even changed our birth dates on their records so we could not be traced. I guess they felt they were doing the right thing by us."

During the nine months the children were at the orphanage, their only visitor was one aunt who somehow found out where they were. According to Nettie, "She wanted to take us, but the orphanage officials insisted we sever all connections with relatives. I do not know what happened in my family to lead to this, but it must have been something terrible. I think it's for the best that Nellie and I had no memory of it."

Boys and girls were kept in separate quarters at the orphanage, so Nettie and Nellie never saw Leon. The twins stuck together. "We didn't want to be apart for a moment," Nettie recalls. "All the girls slept in a big dormitory filled with small beds, and every night Nellie would climb out of her bed and into mine. They tried to get her to stop, but she never did."

Life in the orphanage was sterile. The caretakers were very strict and gave no affection. The children ate at long tables. Nettie has no memory of the food, but many years later both she and Nellie could remember the distinctive smell of the harsh soap used for bathing. The building was heated by steam pipes and Nettie burned her arm one day when she accidentally touched one. Someone put a raw egg on the burn as a form of first aid, but Nettie got a scar anyway. In spite of the hardships, she has happy memories of playing in the snow with sleds, building snowmen, and making snow angels.

NO ONE TOLD THE TWINS, who were then six, why they were being taken from the orphanage to the train depot in Kingston in September 1911. When the train from New York City stopped, the girls were put aboard in a car filled with children. As the train chugged away from the station, the twins left behind not only their parents and relatives, but their brother Leon, who would grow up in the orphanage.

Caring for Nellie and Nettie on the train was Anna Laura Hill, an agent with the Children's Aid Society. "She was a dear woman and we felt comfortable with her, though we had no idea what was going on or where we were going," Nettie says.

Miss Hill put name badges on the girls and gave them slices of bread to eat. Nettie remembers that the train was cold and that she and Nellie huddled

Homes For Children

WANTED

A Company of Homeless Children from the East Will Arrive at

McPherson, Friday, September 15.

These children are of various ages and of both sexes, having been thrown friendless upon the world. They come under the auspices of the Children's Aid Society, of New York. They are well disciplined, having come from various orphanages. The citizens of this community are asked to assist the agent in finding good homes for them. Persons taking these children must be recommended by the local committee. They must treat the children in every way as members of the family, sending them to school, church, Sabbath school and properly clothe them until they are 18 years old. Protestant children placed in Protestant homes and Catholic children in Catholic homes. The following well known citizens have agreed to act as a local committee to aid the agents in securing homes:

Dr. Heaston	H. A. Rowland	C. W. Bachelor
F. A. Vaniman	W. J. Krehbiel	K. Sorensen

Applications must be made to and endorsed by the local committee.

An address will be given by the agents. Come and see the children and hear the address. Distribution will take place at

Opera House, Friday, September 15

at 10:00 a. m. and 2:00 p. m.

This poster announced the train that brought Nettie and Nellie Crook to McPherson, Kansas. ORPHAN TRAIN HERITAGE SOCIETY OF AMERICA

together under a blanket, trying to keep warm. "Back in those days, trains were noisy and dirty," Nettie recalls. "Everything was covered with coal dust. The horsehair seats were rough and hard and there were no lights, so everything was pitch-black at night."

At stops along the way, the children were fed. Sometimes they were lined up and people looked them over. When the train reached Kansas City's Union Station, the twins were put on a bench and told to sing "Jesus Loves Me" to help draw a crowd.

Nettie hated this. "We kids had to be showmen so that people would come around and see what was happening. It was awful having to stand up and say something about yourself."

The twins had begun to understand that when children left with people, they were going to new homes. When people showed interest in the girls, Nettie recalls, "Miss Hill made it clear that, even though it would be much harder to get us a home together, Nellie and I could not be split up. Bless her for that."

After four days on the train, the girls were lined up on the stage of the opera house in McPherson, a small town in central Kansas. They were chosen by L. F. and Gertie Chapin, a childless couple who lived in the nearby village of Canton, where Mr. Chapin had a grocery store. Nettie remembers Mr. Chapin as a nice man who took them fishing and brought them little treats from the store. When he gave them gum, he always warned them to spit it out before they got home because Gertie Chapin forbade the girls to have it. Though he was kind, there was one thing that he did not do for the twins: He did not protect them from his wife. Nettie recalls this time well.

> Gertie was a sadistic woman, very cruel. The abuse Nellie and I suffered took place while Mr. Chapin was at work, and we were warned not to tell him, though he had to know. We were forced to eat whatever she put on our plates, including fish bones. We were whipped with a buggy whip for the slightest infraction. It cut through the clothing on our backs and legs. We had to do extremely hard chores, like carry heavy buckets of water from the well out back. One time, Nellie tripped, breaking a dish she was holding. She received a severe whipping. Gertie never seemed to have any remorse about the way she treated us.
>
> I was the tough one. I tried not to let things bother me. Nellie would cling to me. She was easily hurt. We would hug each other in bed and try to defend each other when Gertie went after one of us. We were sweet little girls who just wanted to be loved, and we tried so hard to be good. We were only six years old.

Finally someone reported the abuse to the Children's Aid Society. Miss Hill, who had accompanied the twins from New York, came to fetch them. Once again they found themselves on a train—this one headed back to McPherson, where they had been selected by the Chapins sixteen months earlier.

Miss Hill found a temporary home for them with James and Mary Darrah, a couple in their sixties with a grown son. Mary Darrah was affectionately called "Aunt Mary" by everyone in McPherson. When Miss Hill announced some weeks later that she had found a permanent home for the girls on a farm in South Dakota, the Darrahs explained that they had grown attached to the twins and asked if they could keep them. Nettie and Nellie had grown

Mother Darrah had this portrait of six-year-old Nellie and Nettie taken shortly after they arrived at her home. NETTIE CROOK ENNS

attached to their foster parents as well, and were thrilled when they were allowed to stay.

"With the Darrahs, we were loved and accepted and appreciated. We just blossomed," Nettie says. The girls became known as the Darrah twins. Mother Darrah had them baptized at the Congregational church. During the service the minister was confused by their identities and switched their names, much to their delight.

The Darrahs lived in a beautiful big home with five bedrooms. Mr. Darrah was ill with a disease that would soon take his life, but while he lived, he was an easygoing man who delighted in the girls and was very kind to them. Mother Darrah was strict but loving. She expected the girls to help with the housework, and she taught them to clean, cook, and sew and to do each of these things well. "She was an excellent manager, frugal and exacting," Nettie recalls. "It was hard to measure up to her standards. I remember one time, I was making a petticoat and I could not get the gathers even enough to suit her. I had to rip them out and redo them three times."

The girls won prizes at county and state fairs. They knew how to garden, make soap, and take care of a home. Both girls were excellent students. Even so, they encountered cruel teasing by other children, and were sometimes the object of criticism by adults because they were orphan train riders. When this happened, Mother Darrah bristled.

"How do you know what kind of blood they come from? You don't know how they will turn out," people would say to her.

"How do you know how your own will turn out?" she would snap back.

The girls spent many happy hours on the farm where the Darrahs' son Jim and his wife and five children lived. They considered the twins part of

In 1916, when they were in fifth grade, Nellie and Nettie put on their best dresses for this special picture. NETTIE CROOK ENNS

the family. The girls knew they were lucky to be with Mother Darrah. "Mother took care of us and she loved us, and we loved her," Nettie says.

The twins were never adopted. Mother Darrah wrote to the Children's Aid Society seeking permission to make a legal claim, but was told that because the girls' parents were still alive, adoption was not a possibility.

WHEN NETTIE AND NELLIE graduated from high school in 1923, they began working their way through college. They also cared for Mother Darrah when she became ill with cancer. Before she died, she told the girls how blessed she was that the two of them had come into her life.

The twins graduated from Kansas State University. In 1930, several months apart, both married. Miss Hill had stayed in touch with the girls since they rode the orphan train and sent each of them a wedding present.

For the twins, marriage meant separation. Nellie lived on the East Coast, and she and her husband, Milton Kerr, had two children. Nettie and her husband, Karl Enns, lived a very different life on a farm in central Kansas; they also had two children. The families stayed in close touch. Nettie and Nellie each became grandmothers, and Nettie became a great-grandmother. After both couples retired, they lived across the street from each other in Albuquerque, New Mexico. Nettie and Nellie spent as much time together as possible.

As adults the sisters reestablished contact with their brother, Leon. He had already found their father, and eventually the twins made visits to New York to meet with him. "He cried over us," Nettie said. "He felt that he had abandoned us and was very sorry. He never told us what had happened to cause the family to split apart."

In 1997, just before their ninety-second birthdays, Nellie died. Only then

Even when they were high school freshmen in 1920,
Nettie and Nellie enjoyed dressing alike. NETTIE CROOK ENNS

Nettie and her husband, Karl Enns, and Nellie and her husband, Milton Kerr, celebrated their fiftieth wedding anniversaries together. NETTIE CROOK ENNS

did Nettie begin to talk about their experiences as orphan train riders, for Nellie had never wanted their story told. "She just felt we'd been through too much and she didn't want it brought up," Nettie says. "But our families wanted to hear about it. I don't know if it's better to remember or forget the hard things that happened to us in our lives. Mother Darrah made up for much of the bad, and we both had long, happy marriages. Miss Hill made certain that Nellie and I were kept together, and that was the best thing. Without my twin, everything would have been much different for me."

Nettie Crook Darrah Enns, age ninety-five, was interviewed from her home in Albuquerque, New Mexico, in February 2000, shortly after her husband's death and before moving to her daughter's home in Tempe, Arizona.

CHAPTER 4

Blessed by Six Parents

Sister Justina Bieganek, Rider to Minnesota, 1913

IT WAS THE WORD *sierota* that puzzled young Edith the most. When family friends came to visit, she would usually hear that word used to refer to her. Sometimes a member of the family said, as a term of endearment, "my little *sierota.*"

Eventually she understood the Polish word to mean "orphan," but she did not know what that had to do with her. Several classmates tried to enlighten her when she started school. "Your mother and father aren't your real parents," they said. She took that one straight to her mother, Mary Bieganek (pronounced be-GONE-ik), who told her in no uncertain terms, "*I* am your mother." A strict, very firm woman, her tone of voice told Edith not to ask again.

But she brooded. She would lie awake at night wondering why she had such old parents. Why was she so much younger than her seven brothers and one sister? Why was she the only member of this large family of dark-haired, dark-eyed people to have blond hair and light eyes? Why did a stranger from

John and Mary Bieganek already had a large family when they adopted little Edith, who came on a baby train from the Foundling Hospital. SISTER JUSTINA BIEGANEK, O.S.F.

New York visit the family at its farm near Holdingford, Minnesota, every year, asking questions about her? And most of all, why was she sometimes referred to as an orphan? *Was* she an orphan?

Edith was seven in 1919 when Mary Bieganek fell ill with cancer. On her deathbed, she called her four youngest sons to her bedside and told them that the first one to marry must take Edith because their father was too old to care for so young a child. At the Catholic wake, held in the family home, Edith's brother Joe lifted her up so she could kiss her dead mother on the forehead and say goodbye. Edith never forgot the grief of that moment.

Eight-year-old Edith served as flower girl when her brother Joe married his teenage sweetheart, Rose, in 1920. SISTER JUSTINA BIEGANEK, O.S.F.

She adored her older siblings, but she was most attached to her father, John, who had always doted on her. After her mother's death, she clung to him, following him everywhere. Then her brother Joe married his seventeen-year-old sweetheart, Rose, and they moved into the family home. Eight-year-old Edith was the flower girl in their wedding. Everyone remembered Mary's words. Rose was willing to assume the parental role, and told Edith that she was to address her as "Mother" and Joe as "Father."

Edith found this very hard to do, but Rose was insistent. So Edith began calling her brother "Father," while trying to figure out what to call her real father, and the teenage Rose "Mother," even as she remembered her real mother. Later her elderly father remarried and moved away. Edith keenly felt his loss in her daily life.

Joe and Rose were very good to her and loved her as their own. Eventually Rose would give birth to fourteen children. As the family grew, Edith was needed more and more to help out. The family lived first on one small farm and then on another, and while they had what they needed, there was no extra money. Joe was in poor health, and Edith often helped with the outside work as well as the housework. She attended Catholic school, and everyone went to church regularly. The parish priest was a close friend of the family.

When Edith finished eighth grade in 1925, Joe and Rose considered her education complete. That was all the schooling that most girls got in those days. Now they expected her to help out at home until she married and started her own family. But Edith did not want to marry. Though she did not know what, she wanted to do something different with her life. She loved Joe and Rose and the children, but she was full of questions and longings and uncertainties. She would stare at her white-blond hair in the mirror, gauging how different she looked from the rest of the family. The more she wondered about these things, the more withdrawn she became, convinced that no one in the world understood how she felt.

It was the parish priest who suggested she attend high school at the Franciscan Sisters convent twenty-five miles away in Little Falls, Minnesota. They ran a boarding school. Students like Edith without money could work for their tuition, room, and board. Edith wanted to go, and to her relief, when she asked Joe and Rose, they agreed.

THE CONVENT SCHOOL WAS a whole new world for Edith, who was then eighteen. After years of living and working on the farm, she loved being back in school and experiencing a new place with new people. She worked in the convent nursing home, taking trays to patients and helping with other tasks. It thrilled her to be around the nuns, so accepting, quiet, and devout. She often had long chats with her favorite, Sister Mary Catherine, who suggested to her that she consider joining the sisters' community. Edith was deeply happy at the prospect of a life of service and devotion, doing God's work.

In 1929 she took her vows in the Franciscan order, becoming Sister Justina. Now she had yet another new family—one with three hundred sisters. She embarked on what would be a forty-year career as a teacher of religion and music. She lived in Arizona, Wisconsin, and Minnesota, eventually settling into the convent at Little Falls, Minnesota.

All those years, she never stopped wondering about her identity. "I tried to get family members to tell me what I felt I had a right to know, but nobody would," she says. "This had angered me as a child, and it still angered me. More than anything in the world, I wanted to know who I was."

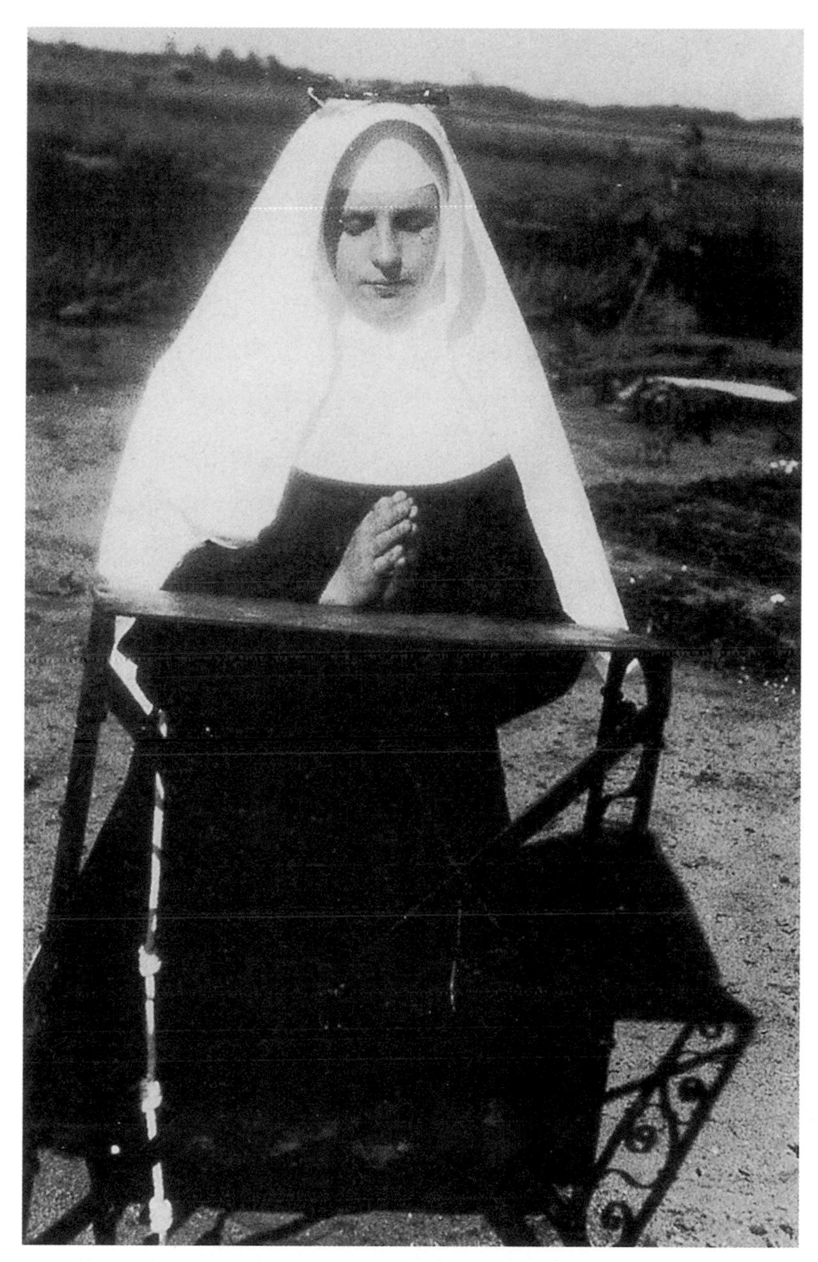

Edith posed for this photo the day she took her vows and became Sister Justina.

Sister Justina Bieganek, O.S.F.

Then, in 1969, she was invited by the Sisters of Charity at the New York Foundling Hospital in New York City to attend the Foundling Hospital's one hundredth anniversary. According to the invitation, she was invited because she had once been a resident of the Foundling. *So that was where she had come from!*

Sister Justina immediately wrote, asking for information about records and how she had come to be there. Sister Miriam Augustine of the Foundling staff responded, but would only say, "Your mother loved you and could not care for you."

Sister Justina felt that she was getting somewhere at last, but she was far from satisfied. She wanted to know if she been abandoned, and if her mother had been married. She wanted to know if she had siblings. She started the search for her birth certificate, writing to several New York agencies. No one could locate it. She wrote again, and then again. Finally a clerk began checking dates other than the January 18 date she had given, and found the birth certificate under January 16.

For fifty-seven years she had celebrated the wrong birth date!

If more could be found out, she had to know. She could not wait for the July 1969 anniversary celebration; she began making immediate plans for her first visit to New York City. The sisters greeted her warmly, delighted that she was a nun like them. Her first evening at the Foundling Hospital, tiny Sister Miriam Augustine, with whom Sister Justina had corresponded, casually said that she would show her the closed-records room. In rapid succession, she unlocked the door, ushered a stunned Sister Justina into the room, and seated her before a microfilm-reading machine, telling her to stay as long as she liked. Then Sister Miriam left, locking the door behind her.

In the silent room, Sister Justina stared at the machine. Shaking, hardly daring to hope, she began to study the document displayed on the small screen.

It was her personal file. *Her file.* Edith Peterson, infant daughter of Rebecca Shmidt Peterson, age twenty-six, from Norway, and Magnus Peterson, twenty-eight, a New Yorker, who had died several months before his daughter's birth. The mother had previously given birth to another child. And there was the official paper stating that on February 5, 1912, Rebecca Peterson surrendered her three-week-old daughter to the sisters at the Foundling Hospital.

"How can I express what I felt as I read about myself? I was so overwhelmed," Sister Justina says. "What I had wanted all my life I was now finding. It was only fragments of information, but it told me who I was, and that was enough. This is what every orphan wants. It was such a gift. I have no words to express it."

When her eyes focused on the line where her mother had signed away custody, her heart skipped a beat. "Seeing Mother's signature come up on the screen was something I will never forget. She was real to me. She was my mother. I knew in my heart that this was the closest I would ever get to her. I traced my fingers over that sacred writing on the glass screen, and as I touched it, I felt I touched her. Something happened. In that moment, I found inner peace."

As Sister Justina read through her file, she learned that John and Mary Bieganek had written to the Foundling Hospital from their Minnesota farm home, saying that they would like to adopt a two-year-old girl and wished for one with blond hair and blue eyes. Matching their request with the exception of eye color—for hers were hazel—little Edith Peterson, then twenty-two months old, was placed aboard a baby train with fifty other Foundling

Hospital children on their way to new homes. The number forty-one was pinned to her, the same number given to John and Mary, who came to the train station on the appointed day to meet their new daughter. When John Bieganek first spotted her, he commented, "I hope she's number forty-one!" and seeing that she was, he scooped her into his arms.

The file included their letter of application, along with correspondence between the Bieganeks and the sisters. John and Mary never mentioned why, at their ages and with their large family, they wanted to take an orphan child—something Sister Justina still wonders about. But they always said in their letters to the sisters how happy they were with their new daughter.

Throughout that evening and the next as well, when Sister Miriam Augustine once again unlocked the records room door and left her alone, Sister Justina copied by hand every word in her file, making sure she had every comma and period exact. Afterward, before thanking Sister Miriam for what she had done, she asked if there was any information on her sibling. There was none.

When Sister Justina returned to Minnesota, she felt reborn. Her resentment and anger were gone. Then she began to research the orphan trains.

I learned how extremely difficult conditions were in New York City in the early 1900s. When Mother was widowed, she was only twenty-six and she had two children. All I have to do is put myself in her situation. Perhaps she had no means of support. I believe that surrendering me was an act of love. The document gave as her reason, "inability to care for the child." She might have been sick and had to give up my sibling as well, or perhaps the two of

When Sister Justina celebrated her fiftieth year as a Sister of Saint Francis in 1979, she was joined by several very special friends — orphan train riders Margaret Washtock, Marge LaMoure, Mary Buscher, and Anne Lemke. SISTER JUSTINA BIEGANEK, O.S.F.

them went back to Norway. The document also said I was in excellent health, so I believe she had given me loving care.

Sister Justina learned of a reunion held in Minnesota every year since 1960 for Minnesota orphan train riders. In 1970 she attended, and for the first time in her life she was among other adult orphans. "They all understood how I felt," she says.

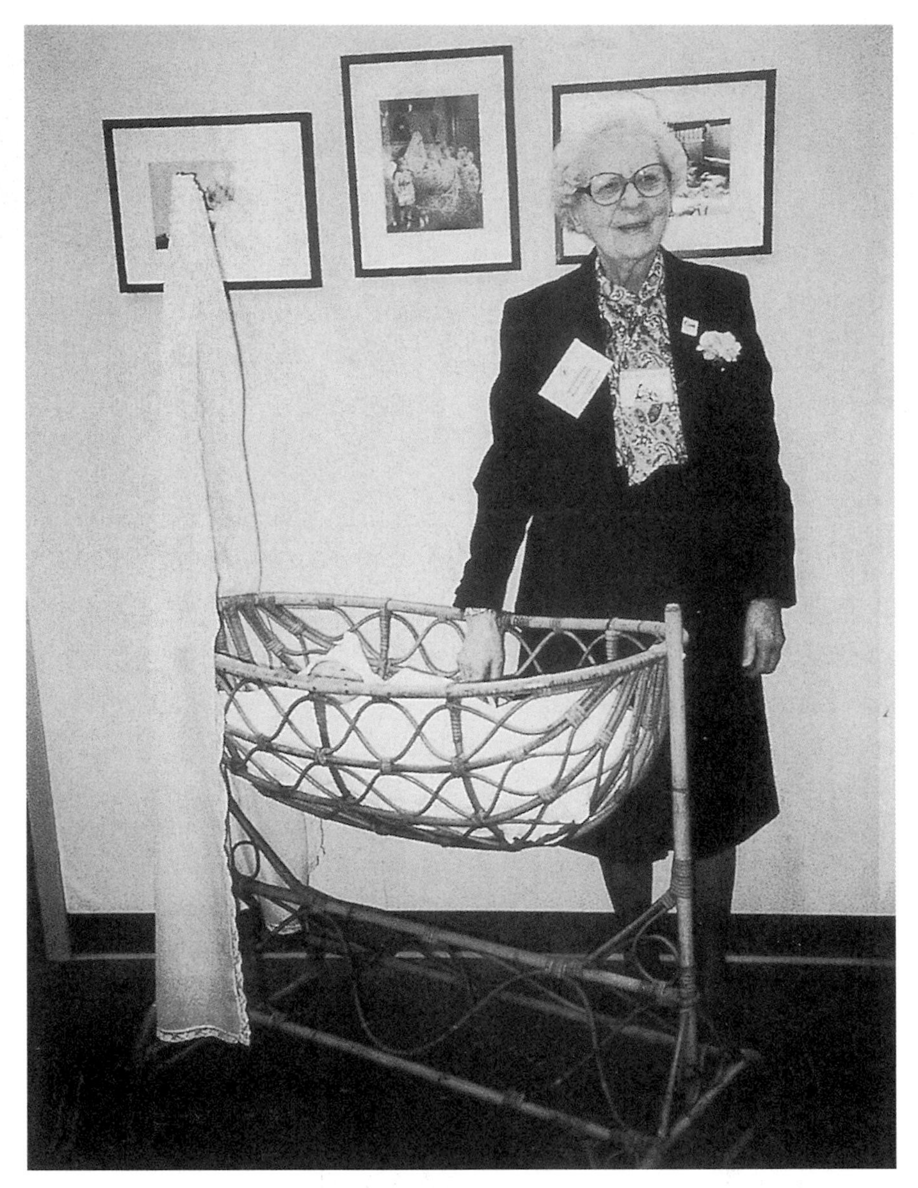

At the summer 2000 reunion of orphan train riders in New York City, Sister Justina was very moved when she saw the replica of the original cradle that stood in the vestibule of the Foundling Hospital where mothers could anonymously leave their babies.

SISTER JUSTINA BIEGANEK, O.S.F.

For the past ten years, Sister Justina has hosted the annual reunion at the convent. "One thing we have in common is that many of us had our identities hidden from us when we were children. I believe this is wrong," she says. "It is possible that I was shown my records at the Foundling Hospital simply because I am a member of a religious community. Many others who were at the Foundling have requested the same access and have been denied. That is not right. They are equally entitled."

Today Sister Justina continues working in the music center at the convent. She is much loved by her Minnesota family and by her convent community. Every morning she talks to her birth mother in prayer. "I hold her very close to my heart," she says. "I ask God's blessing on Rebecca and Magnus Peterson, on John and Mary Bieganek, and on Joe and Rose Bieganek. They are all my parents. Each helped bring me to where I am."

Edith Peterson Bieganek, now Sister Justina Bieganek of the Franciscan Sisters of Little Falls, Minnesota, was interviewed from her home at Saint Francis Convent, in February 2000, when she was eighty-eight.

CHAPTER 5

A Lonely Little Girl

Ruth Hickok, Rider to Iowa, 1917

RUTH HICKOK WAS NOT quite two when her father deserted the family in 1914. He left behind a desperate young wife who had no way to support Ruth and her baby sister, Evelyn. Like her husband, Ruth's mother was an immigrant from Norway. She spoke very little English. She was living in New York City, perhaps in an overcrowded slum, without friends or family to assist her. How could she feed and care for her children?

Ruth has only bits and pieces of information about her first years of life. She knows that in 1915, when she was three, her mother put her in an orphanage and then went to work as a live-in housekeeper. She was able to keep baby Evelyn with her for as long as she was nursing.

"But they would not allow her to bring a second child," says Ruth, "and the best guess is that she later had to give up Evelyn. Only God knows what happened to my sister."

She has fragments of memory about the orphanage, a large stone building in Brooklyn. She remembers little children crying and rows of white iron beds. She was not mistreated, but she received little individual attention from the busy staff. She knew only Norwegian, but gradually learned enough English to understand what was going on around her.

Orphanage life was bare-bones. Ruth had nothing that was actually hers. Clothing, shared by all the children, was patched and mended until it fell apart. The few toys available to the children were in poor condition. Older children were expected to help care for the younger ones. No holidays were celebrated. There was never quite enough food, and bigger kids routinely snatched food from the smaller ones.

Ruth was four when her mother visited her for the last time. She was told that her mother was sick and that they could not touch each other. Ruth cried. She thinks now that her mother might have had tuberculosis, which was widespread at that time. This would explain why her visits stopped—and why she gave her permission for Ruth to be put on an orphan train.

However it came about, in 1917 when she was five, she boarded a train with forty other children. She and a four-year-old boy were the youngest. Clara Comstock was the agent accompanying the band of riders. Ruth remembers her as stern but always kind to the children.

Ruth mainly recalls the food she ate along the journey. "We lived on mustard sandwiches. Just bread with mustard on it, nothing else," Ruth says. "We got sick of it, but we ate it, or we went without."

One day the conductor came into the car with a bushel of wormy apples. He told the children they could throw them out the train windows, so that the seeds would grow into apple trees along the tracks. Ruth remembers with delight how the windows were opened and the children hurled the apples with all their might.

The train's final destination was to be Minneapolis, with stops along the way where prospective parents could view the children. Miss Comstock did not explain to the young riders what was happening, and it took Ruth a long time to understand that all those people looking over the children were picking them out to take home. By the time the train reached Forest City, Iowa, she still had not been chosen by a family. Perhaps it was because her English was poor, or perhaps because she was too small to be able to do much work.

The children were marched from the train depot in Forest City to a local church for viewing. Ruth's shoes were too small and pinched her feet. It was difficult for her to walk, and she lagged behind the others. When the children reached the church, they were each given one cookie. They wolfed them down.

This time, two different couples wanted to take her with them. Somehow a decision was reached and Miss Comstock took Ruth to the home of the couple selected to get her. When Miss Comstock left, Ruth began to cry. "I was away from the other kids and I was in a strange house with a strange woman. I was very hungry and I was exhausted from the trip," she recalls.

> Well, that woman shook me hard, trying to get me to stop crying. I was so frightened, I could not stop, so she spanked me and then slapped me. I had never been treated like that and it just made me cry harder. She said I would get no supper until I stopped. But I couldn't.
>
> So she put me in the cellar and locked the door. It was very dark and smelled musty and was cold. I clung to the steps in fear, crying hysterically. Finally I passed out, probably from exhaustion and hunger. The next thing I remember is waking the following morning on her kitchen floor. The

Newly arrived in town, with the selection process about to begin, these orphan train riders must have felt both excited and scared. PRIVATE COLLECTION OF ANNA LAURA HILL, COURTESY OF THE ORPHAN TRAIN HERITAGE SOCIETY OF AMERICA

doorbell rang and the woman went to answer it. I heard Miss Comstock's voice and ran to her and wrapped myself around her legs and hung on for dear life. I was not going to let her get away from me.

Miss Comstock realized that something was very wrong. She told the woman that it did not look like the placement was going to work out, and to get my things. As we walked through town, me limping along with my pinched toes, I told Miss Comstock what had happened to me. To this day, I dislike cellars and basements.

We stopped at the local café so she could get me washed up. Somebody there gave me a glass of milk. I had not had a thing to eat since the day before when I got that cookie, and I still remember how good that milk tasted.

Miss Comstock took Ruth to Ted and Nattie Jensen, the other family who had wanted her. Ted Jensen owned a wagon business. They lived in a large house painted white that had a yard with big trees. They had two sons, ages eight and eleven. (Later they had a third son.) Two unmarried aunts also lived with them, one of them named Agnes. Ruth's name up to that time had been Agnes, but because of possible confusion, the family suggested she change it to Ruth. She agreed.

When everyone sat down to eat, Ted Jensen told his new daughter she needed to take her arms off the table. "I said, 'But there are long fingers.' At the orphanage I had learned to protect what was on my plate by shielding it with my arms, and to eat fast. My new father understood. He said, 'Oh no, there are no long fingers in this house.' I thought about that. I said, 'Are you sure?' And he smiled and said, 'I am sure.' Then I looked at my new mama, who had put more food on my plate than I had ever seen before, and I asked if it was all mine. She assured me that it was. So I moved my arms and ate everything they gave me, plus more."

Her new mother and aunts set to work making clothes for her. Their first

When Ruth Jensen went off to school, her mother and aunts made sure she was one of the best-dressed children there. RUTH JENSEN HICKOK

project was a nightgown. "It had pink and blue flowers and I thought it was the most wonderful thing I had ever seen. I kept it long after I had outgrown it. I kept saying, 'Is this really all mine?' I had never had clothing of my own, and certainly nothing so fine as this. I could not believe it."

When Ruth started school a few days later, she was one of the best-dressed children there. She also had new shoes—ones that fit well.

But even a cute five-year-old with blond curls and beautiful clothes could not overcome the prejudice of some townspeople. To many in Forest City, Iowa, she was always "that girl the Jensens got off the train." Growing up, she would occasionally hear from somebody, "Oh, you're that orphan girl, aren't you?" One adult actually told her she was a "nasty girl," another that anybody from an orphanage was dirty, a troublemaker, and could not be trusted. Some children were not allowed to have anything to do with her.

Her first Christmas with the Jensens, just a few months after her arrival, was a mixture of good and bad. The lit candles on the Christmas tree frightened her because of memories she had of a fire at the orphanage, and she refused to go into the room where it stood. Her father carried her in to see the tree, then blew out the candles to ease her fears. She could hardly believe her gifts—a beautiful doll and a pink organdy dress.

But at the Sunday school Christmas pageant, one mother protested having "that orphan" in the choir with the other children. The teacher, who liked Ruth, solved the problem by giving her a solo to sing and a special place to stand.

Sensitive about her status as an orphan train rider, Ruth kept to herself. She got along well with her brothers, but had few friends. "I knew one other girl in town taken from the train that same day as me, but for some reason—

I never knew why—the family sent her back to the orphanage when she was twelve or thirteen. The other kids chosen that day lived on farms and I rarely saw them."

School was difficult for her, and this, too, affected her self-confidence. "Starting out, I had language problems because I did not know English well," Ruth recalls. "But my real problem was that my vision was poor. My mother expected me to be self-reliant to the point that if I complained about something, I was expected to 'overcome' it on my own. I could not overcome poor vision. I did not see an eye doctor until I was an adult. Glasses would have made a real difference for me as a child."

One of her great joys was Sunday school and church. In the orphanage she had been taught to say her prayers and always found solace in religious services. "The Jensens were not churchgoing people, but they didn't mind that I went. My faith has helped me get through the hard times."

When she was a teenager, Ruth met Orville Hickok on a blind date arranged by a friend. For several years they dated steadily. They were married in the Jensen living room in August 1931, when Ruth was nineteen.

It was the time of the Great Depression, and money was scarce. Orville worked for the railroad. They lived in a house on a farm owned by Orville's relatives and stretched their pennies to meet expenses. In spite of the financial difficulties, those were happy years for Ruth. She and Orville had a son and a daughter and were married almost sixty years before Orville died of cancer. He was the love of Ruth's life. "He was a Christian man, a special man, and we had a good life together," she said.

Today Ruth has grandchildren and great-grandchildren who give her

Ruth met her husband, Orville, on a blind date when she was a teenager and never dated anyone else. RUTH JENSEN HICKOK

much joy. She has not been able to achieve one lifelong desire: finding her younger sister, Evelyn. She started her search in earnest once her adoptive parents had died, writing letters to the Children's Aid Society and state agencies in New York. She was able to learn a little more about herself and her birth parents, but Evelyn's fate remains a mystery.

Ruth and Orville commemorated their fiftieth wedding anniversary with a celebration and this special portrait. RUTH JENSEN HICKOK

Ruth began to give talks about the orphan trains and always mentioned her missing sister, hoping someone might have a clue for her. She believes that Evelyn was placed in an orphanage and then put on an orphan train and sent west, just as she had been. Several times in her adult life Ruth has met people who have mistaken her for someone else or said that they had once seen a woman who looked almost identical to her.

After years of trying to find her sister, Ruth turned to God in prayer. She would say, "Lord, I'm not getting anywhere with this. If you want me to find my sister, you're going to have to arrange it." Today she is philosophical about her search. "I haven't found her, so apparently the answer was, 'Wait until you get to heaven.' I am content to do that."

Ruth Jensen Hickok, whose birth name was Agnes Anderson, was interviewed from her home in Titonka, Iowa, in January 2000, when she was eighty-eight. She later moved to Garner, Iowa.

CHAPTER 6

The Baby in the Basket

Art Smith, Rider to Iowa, 1922

WHEN ARTHUR FIELD SMITH was growing up, he spun fantasies about the birth mother and father he never knew. Because he had musical talent and also loved acting, he decided that his mother had been an actress and singer in New York City. He dreamed that she had married a young soldier who was killed in 1917 in World War I, a few months before Art was born. "I believed that she loved me very much, but that she died tragically following my birth," Art says. "This little scenario was somehow comforting to me."

His last name was Field, and whenever he encountered someone with that name, he would wonder if they might be related. He continued to wonder this until he was seventy-one years old.

The first years of his life, he lived in a succession of foster homes. When he was five, his custody was transferred from the welfare division of New York to the Children's Aid Society, and Art was informed that he was going west to find a family. "I was scared, but I was also excited," he recalls. "They told me I would like having parents of my own."

He was dressed in new clothes and put aboard a train in New York City with eleven other orphans for the ride to Clarinda, Iowa. Clara Comstock was the agent in charge. She had already made arrangements with a committee of prominent Clarinda citizens to receive the children, and therefore planned no other stops along the way. Her friend, agent Anna Laura Hill, was along to assist, and so was Mary Reynolds, a nurse. Art remembers little about the trip, except that the children slept in their seats and that they ate fruit, bread, and peanut butter and jelly for their meals.

It took three days for the train to reach Clarinda, and it was a cold day in early December 1922 when the children were taken to the Methodist church. A large crowd was waiting to look them over. Growing up, Art was often told the story of how he approached a man in the audience and asked, "Are you going to be my new daddy?" Art thinks that he was coached by Clara Comstock to say that, for he was very shy. "She was determined to find homes for all of us, and she would try anything that might work," he recalls.

It did work. The man, James Worley Smith, and his wife, Lillian, had come to the viewing out of curiosity. They were in their forties and already had an eight-year-old son. "I guess I plucked at their heartstrings," Art says with a laugh, "because they said they wanted me. And it turned out to be a very good match."

On the Smith farm outside Clarinda, Art was introduced to chickens, milk cows, pigs, horses, and cattle. He saw the barn and sheds, the vegetable garden, and the strawberry patch. His new brother, Cecil, took him to the attic of the big white farmhouse, which was filled with all kinds of toys. Art thought he must be in heaven. Only a month later, on a cold January night, the house

This studio portrait of Art was taken shortly after his arrival in Clarinda, Iowa, at the age of five. ARTHUR F. SMITH

burned down when a chimney caught fire. The family was safe, and they built a new home. But the fire destroyed all of Art's paperwork from the Children's Aid Society.

Cecil liked having a younger brother, and he and Art became steadfast friends. "Cecil loved farming and he loved music," Art says. "He could listen to a song on the radio and then go to the piano and play it. He teased me a lot, but he was a good brother."

Art's new father had grown up in the Tennessee mountains with seven brothers. The family was very poor, and James Worley Smith had come to Iowa looking for work. He started as a hired hand, then rented a farm, and eventually owned his own. "He had no formal education, but he was smart and he was a hard worker," Art recalls.

His new mother was a kind woman who had been a schoolteacher. She was certain her scrawny new son was only four years old, and she wrote the Children's Aid Society to ask. They wrote back, assuring her that he was five. A few weeks later she wrote again, this time reporting, "Arthur seems to be getting along well, but he wakes up at night screaming 'Don't let them take me away from my new home!'"

"Along with being shy and backward, I was small for my age," Art says. "It took time for me to feel secure and to come out of my shell."

His new mother's cooking helped. "She was renowned for her baking," Art remembers fondly. "Pies, cakes, you name it. I have wonderful memories of coming home from school to the aroma of fresh baked bread. Mother would cut off a big slice for me and spread it with homemade jam and homemade butter. It was the most delicious thing in the world."

The Smiths were thrifty, conservative Presbyterians, and they were strict.

This studio portrait of Art and his new brother, Cecil, was taken shortly after Art arrived in Clarinda, Iowa. ARTHUR F. SMITH

"You did what you were told," Art said, "or you'd get a switching. My mother never hurt me, but she used that switch plenty of times."

From the beginning, Art had chores to do. As he got older, he assumed more and more responsibility around the farm. He also had time for play, and he was close friends with Fredonna, the little girl on the neighboring farm. On the day he started school, walking off hand in hand with Fredonna, his mother sat down to write the Children's Aid Society with good news: "He's becoming a regular little farm boy!" she informed them.

Before long, filled with contentment and good food, Art not only lost his undernourished, scrawny appearance, but became chubby. "My family was afraid I would grow up to be a fat little man, but later I shot up to over six feet and I stayed slim after that," Art says.

Every year, Clara Comstock came to check on him, and Art was always glad to see her. "I didn't worry about her visits because I knew my family loved me, especially my mother, with whom I was always great pals."

His cousin, Marilyn Graham, later told him, "I never heard anyone mention that you were an orphan. You were as much family as if our blood was coursing through your veins. I always thought you 'belonged' to Aunt Lilly and Uncle Worley, which you did!"

But as a child he wondered about his past. His parents, who legally adopted him in 1929 and added Smith to his name, would not talk about it. So he kept his concerns to himself. "I think those five years in foster care, being shifted around so much, left me with deep insecurities. I could never quite get past them," he says. "I fit right in with the family, and Cecil and I looked enough alike to be blood brothers, but I always wondered who I was and where I'd

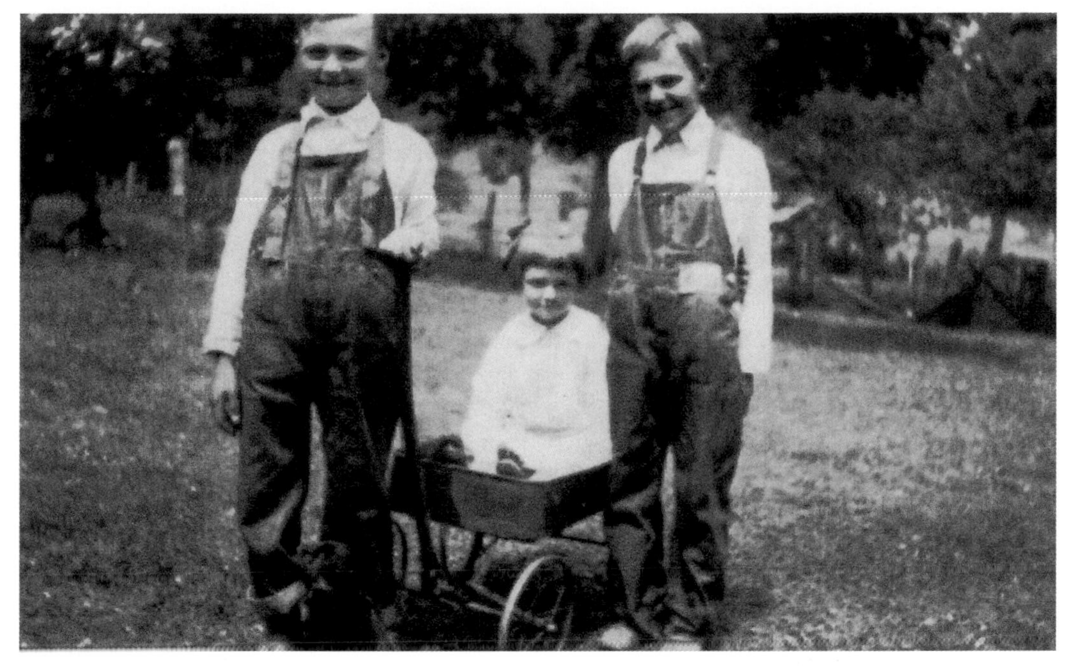

Agencies placing children tried to make sure that each child was visited once a year by an agent. Anna Laura Hill, a longtime Children's Aid Society agent, visited these children at their new home. PRIVATE COLLECTION OF ANNA LAURA HILL, COURTESY OF THE ORPHAN TRAIN HERITAGE SOCIETY OF AMERICA

come from. I didn't forget my fantasies of my beautiful, doomed birth mother and my belief that she had been an actress and singer."

Art loved school and was active in sports, music, and drama. When he graduated from high school in 1936, his mother wrote in a letter to the Children's Aid Society, "I have done all I can for Arthur. He's been very active in school, in church, and on the farm. He has become a fine young man with good habits and many friends. Now, if you can tell me how to get in touch with his birth mother, I'd like to share him with her."

At the time of his high school graduation, Art was an outstanding student and athlete, with special interests in music and theater. ARTHUR F. SMITH

She received no reply. Art learned of her request only a few years ago and is moved to tears when he thinks about his mother's generosity of spirit in hoping to locate his birth mother. "It tells you something special about this beautiful lady who raised me," he says.

THE GREAT DEPRESSION WAS on, and Art wanted to go to college, but money was scarce. After working for a year in a hardware store, he started college classes, holding a part-time job to meet expenses. His mother contributed her butter and egg money and he managed to just get by. During his sophomore year of college, his mother died of cancer. "I was devastated," he recalls.

When World War II started, Art went to officer candidate school. While stationed at Fort Dix, New Jersey, he attended a dance and met Georgianna, a first-year schoolteacher. They married in 1942 before Art was sent into combat in North Africa and Italy.

Their first daughter, Patricia Ann, was born in January 1944. Art was overseas and did not receive word of her birth until she was two weeks old. She was nearly a year old before he was home on leave and could hold her in his arms. "I can't describe to you what it felt like to touch another human who was related to me by blood," he says. "I was no longer alone on this planet. Only an orphan knows what that feels like."

Art was discharged from the army in 1946 after spending eighteen months in a hospital, recovering from a war injury. The family settled in Trenton, New Jersey, and their second daughter, Carole Lee, was born in 1948. Art became a businessman and Georgianna continued teaching school.

The mystery of his origins still haunted him. "It bothered me that I was an orphan," he admits. "I always felt that somehow I wasn't as good as other people because of that fact. One time Georgie and I were invited to join a family celebration for friends. Many of their relatives were there, and in the midst of the festivities, I found myself feeling so lonely, knowing that I had missed this all my life. I, too, had birth family out there somewhere, but I never had the chance to know them."

Art and his wife, Georgianna, have a mutual interest in the orphan trains and try to attend every yearly reunion held for riders. ARTHUR F. SMITH

Art tried several times to get a birth certificate, writing every agency he could think of and giving them what little information he had about himself. But nothing could be found for an Arthur Field born on the date he gave them. He had not needed a birth certificate for the military, nor to begin collecting social security. Then at age seventy he applied to get a passport so that he and Georgianna could travel overseas and was told that he must present a birth certificate. A cousin remembered the name of the law firm that had processed Art's adoption many years before, and he wrote to the firm, asking for any paperwork it had. The information sent back to him included the name of the Children's Aid Society, Art's legal guardian before his adoption.

Art wrote to the society and explained his problem.

The letter he received in reply in December 1988 stunned him. It began:

> Dear Mr. Smith,
>
> Regarding your background, I regret that what I have to say may be painful. On January 12, 1918, you were left in a basket in Gimbels Department Store by a woman who was thought to be your mother. Apparently you had been given good care because you were in good health, and you were wearing clothing of good quality. . . . Efforts were made to locate your parents but to no avail. Therefore you came into the care of the New York City Department of Public Welfare; and they assigned you the name Arthur Field and the birth date of December 2, 1917, and you were baptized Protestant.

Art was crushed. The birth mother he had held in close and loving memory all his life had *abandoned* him, leaving him, a month-old baby, in a department store! His name, Arthur Field, was simply assigned to him, as was a birth date. It was just made up. There was no tragic young actress who had loved him dearly.

"I tried to comfort myself with the knowledge that I had been well cared for, but the truth was, I wanted to crawl into a hole and hide from the world," Art says. "I was probably born out of wedlock—a shameful thing in those days. And then my birth mother took me to a store and left me. I was seventy-one years old when I learned this. I was so upset, I didn't want to talk to anyone about it."

Art often speaks to school classes about his experiences as an orphan train rider.

ARTHUR F. SMITH

Georgianna helped him gradually work through the pain and realize that whatever happened had not been his fault, that he was a victim of circumstances. Art was able to make peace with his past, and to accept that he would never know his own history. He learned enough about the times in which he was born to understand why his birth mother might not have been able to keep him. He gives her credit for leaving him in a place where he was immediately found and cared for.

"Perhaps she thought that a well-to-do woman shopping that day would see me and decide to take me," he said. "She probably could not have known I would end up in foster homes."

Now in his eighties, a grandfather, and still active and healthy, Art is busy promoting the history of the orphan trains. He and Georgianna enjoy going to schools to talk to students about his life. He also works as an advocate for foster children and is a member of the board of advisers of the Children's Aid Society.

One of his special interests is in seeing that all adoption files are opened to adoptees, giving them whatever information exists about them. "For medical and every other reason, orphans have just as much right to know about themselves as everyone else," he says. "Take away the veil of secrecy and let there be light."

Arthur Field Smith was interviewed from his home in Trenton, New Jersey, in May 2000, at the age of eighty-two.

CHAPTER 7

A Case of Scandalous Neglect

Howard Hurd and Fred Swedenburg

Riders to Nebraska, 1925

"My life began when I got off that train in Osceola, Nebraska, in 1925," recalls Fred Engert Swedenburg. "I was six years old. My brother was just shy of four. My mind is a total blank before that day. I don't think the good Lord wanted me remembering those first six years."

Howard Engert Hurd, the little brother who made the trip with him, also has no memory of their home in New York, but remembers a few things about their weeklong ride on an orphan train. "I can recall the hard wooden seats. They got so uncomfortable, some of the kids slept on the floor, even though we had no pillows. I remember we ate sandwiches for most meals. The train stopped a lot and it seemed like we were always getting on or off it."

Neither brother knows how many children started the trip in New York City—perhaps twenty-five—but the ragtag band of homeless waifs traveling west grew progressively smaller as children were selected along the way.

Howard *(left)* and Fred looked apprehensive on the day they arrived in Osceola, Nebraska, and had their picture taken near a tree on the courtyard lawn. The agent on the train, Alice Bogardus, had dressed them in identical sailor suits. HOWARD HURD

When they finally reached tiny Osceola, only seven children were left, including Howard and Fred Engert.

The agent with them, Alice Bogardus, was determined to keep the brothers together. Even though they were cute, chubby-cheeked boys with fair hair and brown eyes, no one had been willing to take them both, and Osceola was the end of the line: either find a home there or go back to New York to an orphanage. Miss Bogardus dressed them in matching sailor suits so that people would know they were brothers. Then all the children were lined up and the crowd that had come to see them started looking them over. "We knew what was happening. We all wanted families," Fred says.

Arthur and Hazel Swedenburg, a farm couple from nearby Clarks, Nebraska, had come to the viewing hoping to find a little girl. They already had a teenage son. "But when Mother saw my big brown eyes, she wanted me, and that was that," says Fred. They were not willing to take two children, however. Miss Bogardus, perhaps sensing the opportunity for Fred, relented, and Fred went with the Swedenburgs.

At the end of the day, two girls were left, and so was Howard. The girls would have to go back, but Miss Bogardus located a family willing to keep Howard until a placement could be found for him near Fred. Finally, three months after his arrival in Osceola, Roy and Martha Hurd brought Howard home to their farm near Stromsburg, Nebraska. He settled in quickly. His new family included an older sister and parents who loved him. Like Fred, he attended country school, went to church, and had regular chores. The Hurds and Swedenburgs knew each other, and though they lived a day's journey apart, they got together whenever possible so that the boys could grow up in touch with each other. The brothers know they were lucky.

"I was always treated just like family," says Fred. "In fact, some family members forgot I'd come on an orphan train. My classmates never mentioned it, either, except when one of the agents from the Children's Aid Society would come by to check on me."

Howard and his new parents, Roy and Martha Hurd, and his new sister, Imogene, sat for this photo shortly after Howard's arrival in 1925. HOWARD HURD

Fred worried about those yearly visits. What if the agent tried to take him back? One year he was out on the playground at recess when the teacher came to find him. "A lady from New York wants to see you," the teacher said. Frightened, Fred ran away, hiding in plum brush down the hill from the school until the agent gave up and left. "She came back later when I was in class and I had to talk to her," he says.

He remembers that one agent drove a Model A Ford. Another took a train

Farm life agreed with ten-year-old Fred and his dog. FRED SWEDENBURG

to Omaha and then hired a taxi to drive to the Swedenburg farm. "Now I realize how hard those agents worked trying to make sure each child was okay," Fred says.

One agent wrote in a report about him, "Fred is a real boy. They think he is pretty noisy but on the whole a very good boy and very lovable."

THOUGH FRED HAD NO trouble over his status as an orphan train rider, his brother Howard occasionally did. "Some kids called me names and put blame on me for things because I was an 'orphan.' I never bothered my parents with it. I figured those kids just didn't know better. What I don't understand is, one of my grandmothers criticized my parents for getting me—yet she had taken a girl from the orphan trains twenty years earlier! I used to see that aunt at family reunions and she was very nice. Still, I remember my grandmother telling my mother, 'You don't know what kind of people he came from.' Well, we'd come from nothing. As both Fred and I eventually learned, our blood relatives were worthless."

In 1939 when eighteen-year-old Howard was trying his hand at farming, several former classmates were enlisting in the navy. Howard decided to join them. He was trained as a medic and spent much of World War II assigned to the Second Division Marines in the South Pacific. Action was fierce. He was wounded twice and has worn a leg brace ever since.

During the war he was also stationed temporarily in New York State. The navy wanted to see his birth certificate, so he wrote to the mayor of Canadaigua, New York, the town where he was born, and asked for help getting a copy of it.

Back came the certificate, which held a surprise: It confirmed that Howard

Howard at age fifteen. HOWARD HURD

was born in 1921, but on the thirteenth of October instead of the thirty-first, the date Howard had always celebrated. That was a mild shock compared with what came next: The mayor wrote that Howard's birth parents were both still alive—and enclosed their addresses.

Howard felt a strong pull. Should he go find them? Yes, he decided. He needed to know who he was, come what may.

He still remembers walking up to the house where his birth mother lived. She opened the door, looked him up and down, and somehow recognized

When Howard enlisted in the navy in 1939, he did not know that he would participate actively in World War II. HOWARD HURD

him. "Hello, Howard," she said. But there was no emotion, no hugs or kisses, no "Nice to see you."

"I couldn't believe she could be so cold," Howard says. "It seemed to mean nothing to her that I was there. She had no curiosity about my life. It wasn't any different than meeting someone on the street."

His birth father gave him an equally cold greeting. Howard met other family members living in the area as well. "They were folks you wouldn't want to know. It would have been a terrible place to grow up. They knew about Fred and me, but offered no explanation about what had happened to us. Nobody cared, nobody said 'stay in touch.' I've never understood it."

Howard was determined to not let it get him down. He had his own family to raise now. He had married a New Yorker, and, when the war ended, he went back to New York and started a cab company. By 1947 he and his wife had three sons. Then she walked out, leaving him with the children.

One day, while driving his cab in New York City, he picked up a young woman who had a bruise on her cheek. Howard could see that she was troubled and started talking to her. Gladys opened up to him. Her husband, an abusive alcoholic, had hit her. She was forced to work to support her family. When Howard found out that she had four children, perhaps he should have run the other way. "But something stirred in me," he says, "maybe because of my own background, or because I was trying to raise three little boys on my own."

With Howard's encouragement, Gladys left her husband. The two of them combined their families and struggled along. Howard was tired of the frenzied life in the city. He wanted his children to have wide open spaces. He missed his family back home. Gladys was willing to give Nebraska a try.

Howard's adoptive parents pitched in to help them. By the time the family stopped growing, not only did Howard and Gladys have his three kids and her four, but together they had another six, including two sets of twins. Howard worked as a truck driver. They stretched every nickel of income as far as it would go. "There were times it was real hard," says Howard, "but we loved all our kids. They knew they belonged to this family. Today we are blessed with thirty-seven grandchildren and seventeen great-grandchildren."

HOWARD'S BROTHER FRED took a different, yet similar path in life. During the hard times of the Depression in the 1930s, he had to quit high school after a semester to help his parents on the farm. He was known as the neighborhood handyman, oiling windmills and doing other jobs people were willing to pay him for. He also worked for the highway department and saved his money until he was able to buy a car.

When he was nineteen, he met Idona, then a high school student. He spotted her in town one day when both of them were with friends. Fred still remembers that she was wearing red high heels. He managed to introduce himself, and soon they were going out. They wrote each other every day while he served as a pilot and mechanic in the air force during World War II, and they were married in April 1944.

As with Howard, the military wanted to see Fred's birth certificate, which he was able to get from the state of New York. It said that his birth name was Fred Engert. Fred had always been known by the name Swedenburg, but his parents had never bothered to legally adopt him. So his father went to a judge and said he wanted to adopt Fred, who was then twenty-four. The judge said, "Art, you can't adopt an adult." Instead, the judge arranged for Fred's name to be legally changed to Swedenburg, solving the problem.

Fred and Idona were married in 1944 during World War II. FRED SWEDENBURG

Fred's little daughter Cindy was with him on a visit to Fred's biological father.
FRED SWEDENBURG

This incident got Fred thinking about his birth family. Like Howard, he wanted to know who he was. He and Idona drove to Canadaigua. They found Fred's birth father first. "He seemed like a decent person," said Fred, "but he wasn't much interested in me. He expressed no regret that he hadn't tried to keep us boys."

Fred found out where his birth mother lived, and he and Idona went to the house. Something stopped him from knocking on the door. Maybe it was the indifferent way he had been treated by his birth father. Instead of stopping, Fred drove on. He parked the car downtown, and he and Idona talked about it. Should he go back and knock on the door? What if she refused to see him? *What if . . .*

A policeman pulled up then and told them they had to move the car. Still unsure what to do, Fred started the motor—and drove out of town.

"Later, when I found out how she had treated Howard, I was glad I didn't stop," he says. "That was when I realized why we were put on that train in 1925."

When Fred left the military and returned to Clarks, Nebraska, he first operated the Swedenburg Garage and later had a hauling business. He and Idona had three children and now have grandchildren.

After his mother's death, his father gave him a letter she had received many years earlier from the Children's Aid Society explaining why Fred and Howard had come into the society's care. She hadn't wanted Fred to know the details. It said in part:

> The children were removed from their home on account of improper guardianship, the cause being the scandalous neglect of them by their mother. Their father seemed to be a decent sort of man and surrendered them legally to this society, feeling that their happiness and their chance in life would be increased thereby, and I think in this he was perfectly right.

"I didn't care to know more. I left it at that," Fred says.

But while he closed the door on his birth family, he was interested in the orphan trains. When riders living in Nebraska began having reunions, he

The celebration of their fiftieth wedding anniversary was a happy occasion for Fred and Idona. HOWARD HURD

Almost seventy-five years later, brothers Howard *(left)* and Fred again posed next to the same tree on the courtyard lawn where they had posed together on the day they arrived in Osceola. HOWARD HURD became an active member of their group. "What happens when we're together is very powerful," he explains. "It doesn't matter what our individual experiences were; we are brothers and sisters because we rode those trains."

FRED AND HOWARD HAVE become closer in recent years. Because of their efforts in promoting the history of the orphan trains, they were jointly given the Charles Loring Brace Award by OTHSA. One of their joint projects is a display on the orphan trains created for the Plainsman Museum in Aurora, Nebraska, that draws thousands of visitors each year.

"People seeing the exhibit talk about how terrible it was that children were put on trains, but I tell them, look at all the kids today who are in abusive homes or are stuck in bad foster homes," says Fred.

"I wish we could put *those* kids on trains and find better homes for them," Howard adds. "The system did its best for my brother and me. I think the orphan trains were a wonderful thing."

Howard Engert Hurd was interviewed from his home in Aurora, Nebraska, in December 1999, when he was seventy-nine. Fred Engert Swedenburg, eighty-one, was also interviewed in December 1999 from his home in Clarks, Nebraska.

CHAPTER 8

A Place Called Home

Bill Oser, Rider to Michigan, 1925

MAMIE NASH OSER KNEW she was dying. Every day the ache in her lungs from her tuberculosis grew worse, aggravated by the gritty air she breathed in the slums of New York City. Caring for three-year-old Marge and one-year-old Billy became more and more difficult. Only a year earlier, in 1922, her husband Frank had died of polio. What would become of her children when she was gone? Who would look after two little orphans in a city full of needy people? She had no close relatives to rely on, and she was so poor, she could leave her precious children nothing.

Marge was a resourceful little girl, independent and strong-willed. Billy, the baby, was easygoing, always smiling—and, because of his age, completely dependent on others for his care. When Mamie heard about the New York Foundling Hospital, she felt her prayers had been answered. She went to see the Sisters of Charity who ran the Foundling and they assured her that when the time came, she could bring her little ones to them.

Bill Oser was fifteen months old when he was turned over to the sisters' care. Growing up, he could not remember his mother at all. Still, he could imagine the heartbreak she must have felt when she gave up her children. For a while she came to see them. Bill has a copy of one of the letters she wrote the sisters, asking for permission to visit. Then she stopped coming. As Bill would learn many years later, she died in 1924 at the age of thirty-two.

For the next year, the sisters cared for Marge and Billy. Marge was a handful. Even as a preschooler, she defied authority and was extremely stubborn. But she was fiercely protective of her little brother.

When it was clear that no relatives were going to claim the children, the sisters put out the word that they were looking for a family to take them and found a couple in Michigan. So in March 1925, when Bill was three and Marge was five, the sisters took them to Grand Central Station, kissed them goodbye, and put them on an orphan train headed to Michigan. There, they were turned over to their new family, who lived on a small farm. The only thing Bill can remember of his life with this couple is that the farmhouse had a porch, on which there was a child-size potty that he was expected to use. Until the day she died, Marge refused to share with him her memories of that time. Because the home was isolated in the country, apparently an agent of the Foundling did not visit the children the first year. The second year, an agent came to check on them—and immediately took them away.

"The records said very little, just that we were removed from the home due to 'poor living conditions and other unfortunate circumstances,'" says Bill. "Perhaps there was something they didn't want us to know. Whatever happened to us in Michigan, I think it affected Margie. Maybe I was okay because she looked out for me."

The agent took the children back to New York. The sisters at the Foundling Hospital were waiting for them, concerned that Marge was now more difficult to handle than ever. The children ended up with the Dominican sisters at Saint Dominic's Orphanage in upstate New York in 1928, when Bill was almost six and Marge was eight. Because boys and girls lived in separate quarters, they saw each other only at church, on special occasions when all five hundred children at the orphanage were together, and at the high chain-link fence that divided the boys' and girls' playgrounds.

Whenever the nuns let the boys play outside, Bill went straight to the fence and waited. Sometimes his sister was already there. He would grin at her, recognizing in her appearance his own red hair, blue eyes, and freckles. No matter how unhappy Marge was, she always grinned back.

"It's cold out, Billy. Button up that coat," she might say, insisting that he do so while she watched. "You doin' okay? You're so skinny."

"You too, Margie," he would reply, "a real beanpole."

Many days she looked around to see if anyone was watching, then withdrew a wrapped peanut butter sandwich from her pocket and expertly threw it over the fence to him. "Eat it!" she ordered. Bill obliged, grateful for the extra food. Older, bigger boys made sure they got served first at meals, so he did not always get much. Marge stood watch as he ate, glaring at any boy or girl who dared approach the two of them. Few would try, for the children knew Marge and didn't want to tangle with her.

Yet her gentleness with her little brother was boundless. Bill was sure this pleased their mother, whom he imagined watching over them from heaven. He could feel her love. At night in the dormitory, when the other thirty-four boys in the big room were already asleep, he would stare at the ceiling and talk to her:

> It's very cold this winter, Mom. We have lots of snow here at Saint Dominic's. It's not a bad place. The nuns are nice to us, and Margie takes good care of me. I don't see her often since they keep the boys and girls separated, but she does what she can for me. She helps the nuns take care of the babies because then they give her extra food, which she shares with me. You should be very proud of her. I miss you, Mom, and I love you.

Life was hard in the orphanage. People all over the country were suffering because of the Depression. At Saint Dominic's, there was never quite enough food. Bill remembers lots of meals of vegetable stew. Sweets were a once-a-month treat when each child received one three-by-three-inch piece of cake. Sometimes it was given out the same night the children saw their monthly movie, which was usually a western or a film starring Shirley Temple, who was the nuns' favorite.

Each child had a bed, a small chest of drawers, and the clothes on their backs. They received a new outfit once a year, and in between times learned to patch their own clothes. A shoemaker would occasionally come to the orphanage, and the children would line up to get holes in their shoes repaired. The sisters had it no better than the children. Bill knew they made many sacrifices to care for their young charges.

One day when Marge was thirteen and Bill eleven, Marge wasn't at the fence at playtime. She wasn't there the next day, either, or the day after that. Bill kept asking about her. Finally the two nuns he liked best, Sister Rita Frances and Sister Mary Brigid, told him that the nuns could no longer handle Marge and had sent her somewhere else. Not long afterward, they had to break the news that Marge had run away; no one knew where she was. Bill was devastated. "Margie was everything to me," he explains, "and now she was gone."

THE SISTERS WERE THE only family he had now, and if this was to be his home, he would try to make the best of it. Instead of complaining, as many of the kids did, that the sisters were too strict, he appreciated the self-discipline he was learning. He did not protest the nightly prayers, the 10:00 P.M. "lights out" curfew, the required church attendance, the long hours of schooling, or the many chores the boys were assigned to do. Whether he was helping in the dining hall, cleaning buildings, or working around the grounds, he did his best.

He participated in many sports. Like the other boys, he learned to settle his disagreements in the boxing ring. He formed friendships that proved to be lifelong. He was popular because of his Irish wit, his ready laugh, and his love of music, though away from his friends, he was quiet and unsure of himself.

"Most of the boys did not have parents, but they still had at least one relative—maybe an aunt or uncle—who visited and brought them treats," Bill recalls. "I made sure I was friendly with the ones who got visitors. Sometimes their families would bring me something too. When you're an orphan, you learn to look out for yourself."

But with Marge gone, he was lonely in a way the nuns and his friends could not make up for. He felt like the only person in the world who had nobody. In the darkness of the night, with sleeping boys all around him, he poured out his sorrows to his mother. He wondered what it would be like to have a real family, and whether he would ever know.

At Mount Loretto Orphanage, Bill forged lifelong friendships. Bill *(third from the left)* and three friends posed for this photo in front of the orphanage office in 1940. BILL OSER

The years passed, and Bill transferred to Mount Loretto Orphanage on Staten Island to attend high school. When he graduated, he wanted to stay with the sisters, but orphanage policy required him to leave. Saying goodbye was very hard. At eighteen, he was on his own in New York City, a skinny, shy, redheaded guy.

"It was hard," he remembers. "I lived alone and I was lonely. I was also poor. I made twelve dollars a week as an elevator operator and then as a delivery boy, and I could barely get by. I worried about my future."

At age eighteen, Bill had completed his formal education and was on his own.

BILL OSER

Several of his Mount Loretto friends were also trying to make it in the city, and the boys hung out together, creating their own kind of family. Bill stayed in close touch with Sister Rita Frances and Sister Mary Brigid at Saint Dominic's. One day Sister Mary Brigid had an amazing message for him. "I've heard from Marge," she said. "She's there in the city. I have a phone number for you."

IT HAD BEEN NINE years since Bill had seen his sister. He couldn't get to a phone fast enough. "Hearing Margie's voice was one of the happiest moments of my life," he says. "I'll never forget it."

That very day, he went to see her. She proudly introduced him to her husband and their baby daughter. Bill became fast friends with his new brother-in-law. It was he who had convinced Marge to contact Sister Mary Brigid, because he knew how worried Marge was about Bill. "What can they do to you now?" he had said. "You're married. They can't punish you or make you go back to the orphanage. You're safe now."

Bill learned that after Marge ran away from the orphanage, she had supported herself by working as a maid until she met her husband. Like her brother, she had always wanted a home, and having one at last had made her very happy. Bill began spending as much time as possible with his sister and her family, often sleeping on their sofa. After working for a year in a government program, he got a job with the railroad. The first time he went into a sleeping car, a distant memory stirred in him. He felt certain that he had once slept in the upper bunk of a car like this, and that Marge was in the lower bunk. When he first asked her about it, she refused to tell him anything. Finally she said that the two of them had slept in such a car on their

In 1941, was when he was twenty, Bill was reunited with his sister, Marge, and met his niece, Barbara. It was one of the happiest days of his life. BILL OSER

trip back to New York from Michigan when they were kids. But she would say no more.

Bill served in the army during and after World War II and was sent to Europe. While stationed in Belgium, he came across an orphanage run by Belgian nuns. The children, all war orphans, were cold and hungry. Bill went

Bill remained close to Sister Rita Frances. When she died in 1998, he was the soloist at her funeral mass. He had known her for sixty-five years. BILL OSER

back to his unit and began talking about the kids. Soon the soldiers were taking portions of their own rations to the children and doing what they could for the sisters. "Helping the kids was great," Bill said. "Only another orphan knows what it's like to be one."

Back home, Bill resumed his job with the railroad. He also married the sweetheart he had known since before the war. His old friends from Mount Loretto were his wedding attendants. Eventually he and his wife had three sons, and often got together with Marge and her family. At last Bill had his own home—a wife, children, and a house. His family meant everything to him, and he worked hard at being the best husband and father he could be. He still talked things over with his mother in the middle of the night. He stayed very close to Sister Rita Frances. She was so much a part of his family that the children called her Aunt Sister Rita Frances.

When he could, Bill searched for information about his past. The Foundling Hospital finally revealed a little more about his parents, and he was able to locate their graves. He also found two half-sisters from a previous marriage of his father's and enjoyed a close friendship with them until their deaths. Bill's first wife died, and he was once again a lonely man. The happiness he found with his second wife, Anne, helped him through the loss of one of his sons to cancer, and, in 1999, the loss of Marge, who was then eighty.

In 1987 he had seen a magazine article about the orphan trains. As he read, he came to a startling realization: When he and Marge went to Michigan, they had been orphan train riders! He contacted the New York Foundling Hospital to ask if this were so. Yes, he was told, it was. The train they were on was called a baby train, because it was transporting very young children.

Bill set out to learn all he could about the orphan trains. He joined the

Bill and his wife, Anne, share many interests and enjoy their retirement at their home in Elmont, New York, on Long Island. BILL OSER national organization for orphan train riders and started giving talks about his experiences. Sometimes he was asked why the sisters didn't find another home for him and Marge, as they did for other children whose first placements did not work out.

It could have been that the sisters wanted to keep us together, and they could not find anyone who would take us both. Nobody could handle Margie. As much as I idolized her, I know how difficult she was. She just would not accept being confined in an orphanage.

She never wanted anyone to know we were orphans, and became upset if I asked her about our experiences in Michigan. But what happened to us was not our fault. I'm proud of what I am. And I'm lucky I had Margie and the kind sisters to take care of me. I knew I was loved.

Someone once commented that I must have been raised by good parents. I said, "No, but I was raised by good people." I also believe I've had my dear mother and the good Lord watching over me.

William Edward Oser, "Bill" to family and friends, was interviewed from his home in Elmont, Long Island, New York, in February 2000, at the age of seventy-eight.

CHAPTER 9

The Cutest Child in Kentucky

Betty Murray, Rider to Kentucky, 1930

FOR THE KING FAMILY, getting by was always a struggle. Delia, the mother, was only fifteen in 1909 when she met Tom King, a thirty-year-old rodeo rider who, along with his brother, had started the first traveling rodeo in America. Tom King gave Delia's father $150 for the privilege of marrying her. Within a year they had their first baby, and one followed another. By the time Betty was born in 1925, they already had Bob, Louise, Virginia, Roy, Tommy, Evelyn, and Carl. The girls all had platinum blond hair. Betty, who had big brown eyes, was especially pretty.

With a growing family to provide for, Tom King quit the rodeo and tried farming a little place in Missouri. It was a struggle, and sometimes he worked for the railroad to make extra income. One day in 1927 he decided not to come home.

Delia had no education and no money. She just had eight hungry kids. For a few weeks they managed to get by. Then the local banker showed up and told her, "Your husband sold the farm and the new owner wants to move in. You've got to leave."

The only place Delia could think to go was to her sister's in Louisville, Kentucky. She knew she couldn't show up with eight kids, so she sent Bob to live with a relative in Oklahoma, and found someone else to take Louise and Virginia. Somehow she managed to get to Louisville with the five youngest.

With three children of her own, her sister was not happy to see them. When Delia went out to look for a job the next day, the sister and her husband loaded Delia's kids into the car and took them to an orphanage in nearby Lyndon, Kentucky. When Delia returned that evening, they told her that the children had "gotten lost."

"Now, you'd think that would have driven her crazy, wouldn't you?" says Betty. "Five children, ages nine and younger, simply gone. But from what I know, I feel sure she was glad to get rid of us. She breathed a sigh of relief and got on with her life."

Betty was not yet three and doesn't remember these events, nor does she remember much about the orphanage. Later, whenever she was asked what they ate there, she would always reply, "Oatmeal, oatmeal, no cream or sugar."

She remembers poverty—rural Kentucky was headed into the Great Depression in 1929, along with the rest of the country. The orphanage felt like a prison to Betty because she was kept with the youngest children, separate from Evelyn and the three older brothers she adored. A stern old lady with gray hair ran the place. "I don't recall kindness or smiles. Evelyn took care of me whenever she could, and all five of us would try to find each other and be together whenever we were allowed on the playground."

THERE ARE NO RECORDS to pinpoint dates, but sometime in 1930, when the five King children had been at the orphanage over a year, they were bathed and dressed in clean secondhand clothing. So were several dozen other orphanage children. Eight-year-old Evelyn tried to help Carl, six, and Betty, who was now five, get ready. Roy and Tommy took care of themselves. Betty's light blond hair was trimmed in a pageboy cut, and she was given a boy's camel-haired coat and hat to wear because there was no coat and hat for a little girl.

Then the children were taken to the local train station. Everything was smoke, noise, and confusion, but Betty realized enough to know that her beloved Roy and Tommy were being put on a train going one direction, while she and Evelyn and Carl were placed aboard a train going the other direction. "We cried a bucket of tears over being separated, but the trains pulled away and nobody paid any attention to us," Betty recalls.

Betty's westbound train stopped at little towns along the way. Each time it did, the children were lined up. The gray-haired old lady would talk about them, and people would look them over. Several children would then be led away to make their lives with new families.

When the train reached Owensboro, Kentucky, just a few hours west of Louisville, Betty climbed down the huge train steps, Evelyn on one side of her and Carl on the other.

Confused by Betty's boy coat and hat, a man in the waiting crowd shouted, "Is that a cute little boy?" Betty looked straight at him and replied, "No, I'm a cute little girl." The children were put in cars and taken to the local downtown hotel, an elegant five-story building with a hundred rooms. They rode up the elevator to the grand ballroom. People soon filled it. One by one the children had to step onto a big wooden block so the crowd could see them while the gray-haired lady said something about them. When Betty's turn came, she had to be helped onto the block.

"I still remember what it felt like to stand there with everyone looking me over," she says. "It was awful. It must have been sort of like slaves felt when they were auctioned off."

Afterward the crowd pushed toward the children. Those looking for workers felt the children's muscles and wanted to see their teeth. Evelyn and Carl held on tightly to their little sister. "We all wanted to be picked," Betty said. "But we wanted to stay together."

An elderly couple stopped before the three children and then claimed Evelyn and Carl. "What about my little sister?" Evelyn asked in alarm. "She's too young to milk a cow," the man said, and the next thing Betty knew, Evelyn and Carl were gone. Five-year-old Betty cried and cried, but nobody dried her tears.

The crowd gradually thinned until only a few children were left. Betty was one of them. She had never felt so abandoned and afraid. That was when a handsome, dark-haired gentleman approached and smiled at her. She recognized him from the train station as the man who had questioned if she was a boy. "Would you like to be my little girl?" he asked her. Betty went to his outstretched arms.

With that simple act, she found an enchanting home. Andy Wade was the general manager of the hotel. He and his beautiful young wife, Louise, lived in an apartment in the hotel and ate their meals in the elegant dining room. Maids washed their clothes and did all the housework. Louise liked the idea of a child and readily welcomed this very pretty five-year-old. She loved to dress up her new daughter and saw to it that Betty had dance and piano lessons; she was able to use the grand ballroom to practice. Because Andy and Louise were part of the "country club set" and had many social obligations, Betty had her own nanny. She also had her own room in the hotel and could pick up the phone and order room service whenever she wanted. She had so many toys that some were given away regularly to the Salvation Army. There was even a movie theater across the street where she saw all the latest picture shows. The hotel had some permanent residents, mostly older people, and everyone doted on Betty. All the cooks and waiters and housekeeping staff loved her, and the entire hotel was her playground.

She quickly grew to love Mother and Daddy. Her handsome father was always well dressed, always charming. Whenever music came on the radio, he would sweep her into his arms and dance with her. He also took her to church each Sunday. She even had wonderful, devoted grandparents—her mother's parents—who lived right there in Owensboro.

Betty's mother entered her photo in the "Cutest Child in Kentucky" contest sponsored by newspapers across the state. With her showstopping blond hair, Betty won. Her picture was in all the state newspapers, identifying her as *"Betty Lou Wade, daughter of Mr. and Mrs. Andy Wade of Owensboro."*

But there were also shadows in her new life. Her father had been gassed in World War I and suffered chronic pain. He tried to numb the pain with alcohol, but it grew worse, and so did his drinking. At school the children who teased Betty about being an orphan train rider loved to remind her that Andy and Louise weren't her real parents. Betty became good friends with a boy named Joe who had come on the same orphan train and knew exactly how she felt. Both were ashamed of their pasts. Neither could be adopted by their new families because their birth parents were still living and had not given signed permission.

Twice a year Betty got a hard dose of reality when she went to see Evelyn and Carl, whose new home was a farm twenty miles outside Owensboro. "I was allowed to visit because Daddy was a prominent businessman and the old couple were in awe of him. My brother and sister couldn't be spared from their work to come visit me in town. They were trapped."

Evelyn and Carl lived in a dingy attic room. At 4:00 A.M., seven days a week, they had to milk two dozen cows. Then they started the house and field work. One of their jobs was to pull worms off the leaves of tobacco plants; they often worked in the blazing sun.

"I would show up from my privileged world of private school and fine living," Betty recalls. "We were always thrilled to see each other, but of course they envied me. I felt so bad for them. I brought them gifts, and I always tried to help them with their work, but I never seemed to do anything right."

When Betty was eleven, her world suddenly turned upside down. Unable to tolerate the pain any longer, her beloved father jumped into a river and drowned. He thought he had provided for his family. He did not realize that since his death was a suicide, his large life insurance policy could not be collected. Betty and her mother were left with nothing. For a year they lived with Louise's parents. Betty switched to public school. She worked hard to be the best student she could, but it was a very difficult time for her. "Losing my daddy broke my heart," Betty says.

When she was twelve and finally adjusting to life without her father, everything was turned upside down again. A telegram arrived asking if Betty Lou

Wade was also Gladys Marie King. Betty barely remembered that name—the one she had arrived with on the orphan train. The telegram was from Betty's oldest sister, who had found a copy of the "Cutest Child in Kentucky" newspaper article at the home of the Louisville aunt who had put Betty and her sister and brothers in the orphanage eight years earlier.

"I guess our aunt had seen my picture in the paper and saved it out of guilt or something," Betty says. "Mother telegrammed back that I was the same person, and invited my sister to come visit. I didn't remember her. We went out to the farm where Carl and Evelyn were so she could see them too. We wouldn't have been found if not for that contest."

The following Christmas, 1937, the sister hosted a King family reunion. Betty, Evelyn, and Carl rode the bus to her Indiana home. When they arrived, everyone surrounded them excitedly except a small, hard-looking woman who stayed to one side. She wore a thin cotton dress, heavy work shoes, and men's socks. It was Delia, their birth mother.

Betty went to embrace her, but was pushed away. "She was only interested in a couple of the boys," Betty recalls. "She didn't want anything to do with the rest of us. Here I was, her baby daughter, and there was no hug, no kiss, no nothing. She just didn't care."

Betty had to start all over getting to know Bob, Virginia, and Louise, but she was thrilled to see Roy and Tommy, who were now grown men. She learned that they had both been taken from their orphan train by a tobacco farmer who wanted field help. When Tommy became ill with appendicitis, the farmer refused to pay his medical bills and instead returned him to the orphanage. Once Tommy recovered, he went to find their father, who was

The earliest photo Betty has of herself is her high school graduation picture.

BETTY WADE MURRAY

back in the rodeo business. After that, Roy ran away from the tobacco farm and also joined the rodeo.

Betty's life was a sharp contrast to those of her other siblings. She was the only one who did not have to work and would be the only one to graduate from high school. No one was willing to talk about what had happened to the family, and Betty would never learn much about her brothers' and sisters' lives. They made it clear that they envied Betty and felt it was not fair that her life had been so much easier than theirs.

When Betty returned to Owensboro, she was happy to see her mother and grandparents. She maintained contact with her siblings but would never succeed in having any kind of relationship with her birth mother, who worked as a short-order cook and never remarried. Several years later, during World War II, Betty had finished high school and was working as a secretary. One day her brother Carl contacted her to say he had left the farm and was currently living in Oklahoma with their father, who was laid up with a broken leg. He needed help. Could Betty come?

She thought about it for a long time. Finally she said yes, hoping it meant she would have a father again. But she quickly realized that he only considered her an unpaid housekeeper. For Betty, the memory is painful:

> Even after I'd been there a few months, my birth father still called me "girl." He never used my name. He was always ordering me around. One day when he started in on me, I couldn't take it any longer. "Girl, I told you I don't like my eggs cooked like that," he complained. Well, I'd had it. "You'll eat them however I fix them," I snapped. He got mad and shouted, "Girl, I didn't raise you to talk to me like that!" I just looked at him. "You didn't

raise me at all," I said, and I walked out. I got on the bus that very afternoon. I had enough money for a ticket to Oklahoma City, so that's where I went. I never looked back.

It was 1946 and World War II was over. Betty liked Oklahoma City and decided to stay for a while. She got a job and shared an apartment with three other young working women. They were friends with a group of young men who often met them in a nearby drugstore for sodas. One day a tall, handsome young man just home from the navy was visiting one of the friends and spotted Betty. "See that beautiful girl?" he told his buddies. "I'm going to marry her." "Then you ought to meet her," they declared, and introduced him to Betty. Love bloomed, and indeed they did marry.

THUS BEGAN A VERY happy period of Betty's life. She and her new husband, Dick Murray, had a son and a daughter. They lived in many interesting places as part of Dick's job with the Federal Aviation Administration, including the Panama Canal Zone and a remote island off the coast of Alaska.

Betty was ashamed of being what she called a "throwaway child" and never told Dick or her children about her past or about her ride on an orphan train. It wasn't until a few years ago, when she began hearing about orphan train riders, that she decided to speak up. She learned that many children rode orphan trains from orphanages located in places other than New York, some from one place within a state to another, as she had done. She knew she was fortunate to find a loving family, and that many riders, like her sister and brothers, were taken just to work.

One of the many interesting places Betty and her family lived was a remote island off the coast of Alaska. BETTY WADE MURRAY

Despite hard times, Betty has always maintained a positive outlook on life.

BETTY WADE MURRAY

"I've had my ups and downs. I'm widowed now, and two years ago I suffered a stroke," she says. "But in spite of the bad, I know I've been blessed. I was happily married for thirty-eight years. I've always been very sensitive to other people's feelings and I've always tried to help others. All in all, I've had a real interesting life."

Betty Lou Wade Murray, who was born Gladys Marie King, was interviewed from her home in Ponca City, Oklahoma, in March 2000, at the age of seventy-five.

CHAPTER 10

Into the Future

THERE WILL ALWAYS BE critics of the placing out program who say that the orphan trains were wrong. Yet no better alternative was available at that time. Many orphan train riders have expressed their gratitude for the program.

Robert Peterson was abandoned by his father after his mother died in 1917. He rode an orphan train to Nebraska in 1922 and found loving parents and a happy home on a farm. "We often think of adversity as being a terrible thing, but sometimes it turns out just the other way," he says. "The day I was abandoned on the streets of New York City probably turned out to be one of the luckiest days of my life."

Robert grew up to be a lawyer. He married and had children. Like so many of the riders, he overcame his childhood difficulties and made a success of his life. Countless riders grew up thinking that they were not as good as other people or that they had "bad blood." But they have proved the folly of such thinking. They have shown us how difficult it is for children to be separated

Today, orphan train riders treasure their state and national annual reunions, such as this state reunion in 1998 in Springdale, Arkansas. Whenever riders are together, they feel like family. *Back row:* Mary Ellen Pollock, Fred Swedenburg, Art Smith, Howard Hurd, Jean Sexton, Alice Bullis Ayler, and Margaret Weber. *Front row:* Helen Macior, Harold Williams, Anne Harrison, Marguerite Thomson, Mary Allendorf, Marion Strittmatter, and Helen Davis.

ORPHAN TRAIN HERITAGE SOCIETY OF AMERICA, COURTESY OF HOWARD HURD

from their birth family and how much they long for families of their own. While reminding us of the sensitivity and vulnerability of children, they also remind us of their resilience. The legacy of the riders will live on through their children and through other people interested in the orphan trains.

The problem of abandoned and orphaned children, and children whose parents cannot care for them, still exists in America. More than five hundred thousand children are in foster care, many of them living in homes that are not very good. Some are eligible for adoption. The Children's Aid Society is championing legislation to speed up the adoption process so that adoptable children get into permanent homes more quickly. On other fronts, states are wrestling with the issue of whether to open birth records to adoptees, trying to balance a birth mother's right to privacy with an adoptee's right to know. States are also grappling with abandonment laws that would allow parents to leave infants at hospitals and police stations without being prosecuted as criminals. Such laws, officials hope, would save the lives of unwanted children.

The riders can teach us what it's like to be homeless, to be shifted from family to family, and to be denied access to birth and family records. "We listen carefully to them because we can learn so much from them," says Phil Coltoff, executive director of the Children's Aid Society.

Yesterday's orphan train riders are today's foster children, and they are children who live with grandparents, other relatives, nonrelatives, or single parents. Riders are the children, both American and foreign, who find new families through adoption. They are the children everywhere who are learning, as the riders did, that "family" can transcend biology, that strangers can learn to love each other, and that their bonds as family can be strong and true.

Recommended Reading

Orphan Train Rider: One Boy's True Story (Houghton Mifflin), by Andrea Warren. The history of the orphan trains is interspersed with the story of nine-year-old Lee Nailling, who rode an orphan train to Texas in 1926. Winner of the Boston Globe–Horn Book Award for best children's nonfiction.

The Orphan Train Series (Bantam Books), by Joan Lowery Nixon. Each fictional story is about a different orphan train rider.

Train to Somewhere (Clarion Books), by Eve Bunting. Fictional story about a little girl on an orphan train who is looking for a home.

Orphan Trains, a documentary produced for the American Experience on PBS. Includes interviews with several orphan train riders.

Web sites can be searched using the keywords "orphan trains." For articles about the orphan trains and stories about riders who went to Kansas, check out ukans.edu/carrie/kancoll/articles/orphans.

To request a catalog listing books and other items related to the orphan trains, send two first-class postage stamps to the Orphan Train Heritage Society (OTHSA) at P.O. Box 322, Concordia, Kansas 66901. Phone/fax: 785-243-4471. Email: othsa@msn.com. Or order items through the OTHSA Web site at orphantrainriders.com. This Web site also includes historical information, stories of riders, and articles related to the orphan trains. The orphan train museum at the headquarters in Springdale is open to the public. Phone for hours and directions. Upon request, OTHSA will send students and educators a packet of information about the orphan trains.

Sources Used in This Book

Information for this book was gathered from interviews with orphan train riders and file materials from the Children's Aid Society of New York City and the Orphan Train Heritage Society of America, as well as from the following sources.

Fry, Annette R. *The Orphan Trains.* New York: New Discovery Books, 1994.

Holt, Marilyn Irvin. *The Orphan Trains: Placing Out in America.* Lincoln: University of Nebraska Press, 1992.

"Home at Last." *Hastings (Nebraska) Tribune,* September 29, 1987, p. 9.

Jackson, Donald Dale. "It Took Trains to Put Street Kids on the Right Track out of the Slums." *Smithsonian,* August 1986, 95–103.

Orphan Train Heritage Society of America. *Orphan Train Riders' Stories.* 5 volumes. Baltimore: Gateway Press, 1992–97; Fayetteville, Ark.: Off the Press, 1999.

Patrick, Michael, Evelyn Sheets, and Evelyn Trickel. *We Are a Part of History: The Story of the Orphan Trains.* Santa Fe, N.M.: The Lightning Tree, 1990.

West, Elliott, and Paula Petrik, editors. *Small Worlds: Children & Adolescents in America, 1850–1950.* Lawrence: University Press of Kansas, 1992.

Wheeler, Leslie. "The Orphan Trains." *American History Illustrated,* December 1983, 10–23.

Index

Page numbers in *Italic* type refer to illustrations.